Gourmet Soups

Gourmet Soups

Over 75 original recipes for adventurous and exotic soups

CAROLE CLEMENTS

CHARTWELL
BOOKS, INC.

A QUARTO BOOK

Published by Chartwell Books
A Division of Book Sales, Inc.
P.O. Box 7100
Edison, New Jersey, 08818-7100

This edition produced for sale
in the U.S.A., its territories
and dependencies only.

ISBN 0-7858-0348-3

This book was designed and produced by
Quarto Publishing Plc
The Old Brewery
6 Blundell Street
London N7 9BH

Art Director: Moira Clinch
Design: Design Revolution
Senior Art Editor: Liz Brown
Copy Editor: Alison Leach
Home Economist: Lucy Miller
Picture Researcher: Susannah Jayes
Picture Manager: Giulia Hetherington
Senior Editor: Sian Parkhouse
Editorial Director: Mark Dartford
Photographer: David Sherwin
Illustrator: Carol Hill

Typeset in Great Britain by
Central Southern Typesetters, Eastbourne

Manufactured in Hong Kong by Regent Publishing Services Ltd
Printed in Hong Kong by Sing Cheong Printing Co. Ltd.

Contents

Introduction:
In PRAISE *of* SOUP

*E*very country in the world has its own soup traditions, but it is a universal food. The soup kettle is the great culinary melting pot and the soups in this book come from, or have been inspired by, the traditions of many nations. Some of them combine influences from more than one culture. Learning about the differences and similarities in soup-making around the world has fired my imagination and will, I hope, inspire you equally.

In some measure, the appeal of soup may well stem from its historical importance – undoubtedly it was one of the earliest forms of cooked food when early man harnessed fire. Through the centuries, people needing sustenance, with little else to fill their bowls, put in pieces of bread and ladled over hot liquid. But soup as we know it is much more than that.

Soup is sometimes served as a hearty breakfast, as is the custom in Périgord and in the eastern Mediterranean. Equally, it can provide a healthy and satisfying "liquid" lunch. Historically, the evening meal was soup – *souper*, or supper as we now call it, means "to take soup".

Soup is a perfect multipurpose food. You can dress it up or down, eat it for comfort or to excite the palate. The most versatile dish of our diet, it is welcome in all seasons, popular with all generations. It is great for single people – make a big pot and sip it through the week. And you can readily stretch soup to serve an unexpected crowd. You can also give a new life to leftovers, which provide a traditional springboard to delicious soup-making.

A spirit of improvisation is an asset in making soup. Experiment with what is abundantly available and in season – soup is a good way to make the most of a glut of zucchini from the garden or a whole tray of tomatoes reduced for quick sale at the greengrocer. With a dash of common sense and a pinch of caution, soup can be made from almost anything. Skill and confidence come with practice. Look on these

Endlessly versatile, soup can be prepared from almost anything. This creative aspect makes it as satisfying for the cook as the recipients. Depending on the style, soup may be a light introduction to a meal or a nourishing main course, served up with crusty bread.

recipes as a framework of basic proportions within which you can modify the ingredients to suit your taste and use your own creativity. Some of the most inspired soups have undoubtedly been the result of experimentation.

The recipes in this book all have a little twist – unusual combinations, a novel ingredient, a certain flair in the presentation, an exotic origin, an interesting history. At the same time, these recipes, many of which are essentially quite simple, rely on three basic principles: a preference for fresh ingredients, careful preparation, thoughtful seasoning. All the soups that require stock will taste better if it is homemade. As stock-making requires time but minimal effort, with a little planning it is easy to have available when you want it.

Many soups can be made in advance and may even improve, with reheating, after the flavors have had time to meld. Reheat soup slowly over a moderate heat just until the ingredients are heated through. If some ingredients, such as seafood, are susceptible to overcooking, strain the soup and return them to the pan of reheated soup just before serving. A microwave is useful for reheating, especially for starchy soups that can easily stick.

Serve chilled soup ice cold and hot soup steaming hot. This may seem elementary, but soup can lose its appeal if it is served lukewarm. A tureen will help soup retain its heat, and soup can often be kept warm in its container in a slow oven until you are ready to serve it. Warm or chilled bowls or serving dishes are essential.

Soup can have a place in any part of the meal. A dramatic soup makes an impressive beginning, but it must be light if the main course is substantial, and if the soup is creamy, this precludes another course with cream. Many soups are perfect as a main course, either following a filling starter or as a satisfying one-course meal with the traditional partner, bread. And why not have soup for dessert? Fruit soups can be a light and novel finish to a memorable meal. There are no rigid rules. Use your imagination and go by what you enjoy.

The selection of wine with soup, or anything else, is so much a matter of personal choice that suggestions must be regarded as no more than signposts pointing in a certain direction. The selections in this book represent what I have enjoyed with a particular soup, but ultimately, your palate is the final adjudicator and you must drink what you like. Some people even believe that serving another liquid with soup is inappropriate; others, however, believe that no course is complete without wine. Again, you must follow your own inclinations. Experiment with what you think you might like and what you have available.

Making soup is a creative endeavor. It is rewarding for both the cook and the recipients. The wisps of steam wafting from a soup pot simmering on the stove permeate the atmosphere not just with an aroma, but also with an evocation of hearth, home and history.

The Basics of Soup - Making

OMEMADE SOUP PROVIDES SUSTENANCE AND SATISFACTION IN GENEROUS MEASURE. THE SIMPLE SKILLS NEEDED ARE READILY MASTERED AND THE OPPORTUNITIES FOR PERSONAL CREATIVITY ARE ABUNDANT. SOUP IS THE LIQUID ESSENCE OF ITS INGREDIENTS, EXTRACTED WITH CARE AND RESPECT. THE MOST ELEMENTAL OF FOODS, IT IS ALSO AMONG THE MOST SATISFYING — IT NOURISHES BOTH THE SOUL AND THE BODY.

The BASICS *of* SOUP-MAKING

*S*oup is one of the easiest things to make and homemade soup is worth the small effort it takes. It is as economical as it is appealing, needing no fancy equipment or extravagant ingredients for good results.

Equipment

Soup-making requires very little in the way of equipment, but you will need a large saucepan – a 3l/5pt capacity pan with a lid is really the minimum – or a large, deep enameled iron casserole. If you make stock often, a tall, narrow stockpot with handles (it is quite heavy when filled) is a worthwhile investment. Stainless steel or another nonreactive material such as enamel is advisable to avoid discoloration with acidic and other ingredients that react negatively with certain metals; aluminum is best avoided for this reason. For easy cleaning, stainless steel is excellent.

Sharp knives are essential. You should have at least a paring knife and a long wide-bladed chef's knife, as well as a good-sized chopping board or two, preferably non-porous and dishwasher-proof, and a swivel-bladed vegetable peeler. Kitchen scissors and a cleaver are also useful, as well as various long-handled spoons and kitchen string. All of these you are likely to have in your kitchen already, but you may not have acquired a skimmer, a flat round utensil, perforated or with a wire-mesh insert, used to lift off the scum or froth from stock. For this, a large perforated spoon will also do, but a skimmer makes it easier. For stock-making and for many soups, you will need a strainer and colander. It helps to have several sizes and types: a large fine-mesh wire sieve, a nylon mesh sieve for foods that discolour, a colander for draining, and perhaps a conical strainer and a drum strainer if space and budget permit.

When working with large quantities, a large 2l/3½pt measuring container is more useful than the usual small size. I also find a large capacity fat separator, also known as a degreasing pitcher, invaluable when you need to use freshly made stock and there is no time to chill it and allow the fat to congeal for removal. This is simply a jug with the spout at the bottom so you can pour the grease-free liquid from the bottom and stop pouring when the fat on top reaches the level of the spout.

When a soup is puréed, the smoothness of the result depends on the equipment used: a food mill, food processor, blender or immersible electric hand blender will each process the food in a slightly different way. A food mill is handy because it purées and strains at the same time. It consists of a rotary blade which is turned with a hand crank against a perforated disk, available with perforations of various sizes allowing more or less of the solid matter to pass through. The apparatus is set over a saucepan or bowl, with legs and a handle to steady it. This simple, inexpensive utensil is found in almost every European kitchen and its merits are being rediscovered elsewhere.

The food processor is probably the most widely available electrical appliance today. It produces a purée that is smooth but not homogenous and if there are seeds or fibers, the purée will need to be strained. The most successful technique is to purée the solids with just a little of the liquid, then thin the purée with the remainder of the liquid afterwards, rather than to process several watery batches.

A blender produces the smoothest results. Because the strong suction that draws food to the blades creates a whirlpool effect, the food is homogenized in a way that the food mill or processor is incapable of producing. This is particularly advantageous in many puréed vegetable soups where a silky texture is desirable and even soups made of relatively fibrous vegetables, such as pumpkin, do not need straining after being puréed in a blender. An electric hand blender, a tall wand with small crossed blades like a blender, produces similar results in many instances, and since it is immersed in the cooking pan, cleaning up is easier.

There are advantages and also some drawbacks to each of these appliances. If you are making a large quantity of soup, the relatively limited capacity of a food processor or blender means that puréeing will have to be done in batches, unless you have a professional-sized model. Do not fill the containers more than about halfway. With a processor, liquid may leak around the top and under the blade assembly. With a blender, the suction action creates a cyclone that can push against the lid and lift it even when you are holding it down. It is advisable with either one to allow soup ingredients to cool somewhat before puréeing and to protect yourself from escaping liquid with a towel or oven glove.

Ingredients

Many delicious soups are made with water. It is economical and readily available, and it allows the taste of other ingredients to come through. Although stock can be an important element, there is no need to use stock if a soup has plenty of flavor without it.

Stock is essentially flavored water. It is the cooking liquid of meat, poultry, game, or fish, and/or their bones simmered with vegetables, herbs and water or some combination of these. Meat, poultry, and fish stock add body as well as flavor to soups or other preparations because of the gelatine derived from the bones. A stock made of vegetables and herbs will provide flavor, but not body.

Soup can only be as good as the ingredients from which it is made. Soups and stocks often provide an opportunity to use food that is just past its prime and to give new life to leftovers, but the fresher the ingredients, the more they have to impart, both in terms of flavor and nutrients.

The soup recipes in this book assume peeling of those vegetables which are normally peeled for cooking, such as garlic and onions, and soaking or rinsing of those vegetables that tend to be gritty, such as leeks and spinach. Carrots may be peeled or not, according to condition and personal preference, and potatoes used in soups are generally peeled except for small ones. For stock-making, peeling is not usually essential, apart from vegetables which have been waxed, but all vegetables should be thoroughly scrubbed with a brush under running water. When the zest of citrus fruits is used, unwaxed fruit is preferable; otherwise wash in warm soapy water and rinse well.

Herbs used to flavor soups and stocks are often tied tightly in a bundle to facilitate removal after cooking. This herb bundle, called a *bouquet garni*, usually contains 4–6 parsley stems or sprigs, 3–4 fresh thyme sprigs, 1–2 bay leaves, and sometimes a piece of leek or small leafy celery stalk, but it might also contain herbs appropriate to a particular dish, such as sage, tarragon, or dill. When preparing a large quantity of soup, make a bigger *bouquet garni*, increasing the ingredients and wrapping them in leek greens or bay leaves before securing with kitchen string.

Soup-making requires only simple equipment, most of which will already be at hand in your kitchen. Remember that the best ingredients make the best soups and those made from good quality raw materials, carefully selected and prepared, will have the most flavor.

Stock-Making

*S*tock, the foundation of many soups, is almost effortless to make. It needs more patience than skill and yields a delectable liquid ready to consume as a clear soup or to use as the basis for other soups, transformed with an array of additions.

The French word for stock, *fond*, also means base, foundation – and stock provides the foundation for many soups, as well as some sauces and stews. Stock is easy to make, as it requires almost no attention after the initial stages and

A variety of vegetables and even fruit can be used for stock-making. Adjust the ingredients according to what you have available, but use strongly flavored vegetables sparingly. A stock made without bones needs plenty of vegetables and herbs for good flavor.

virtually cooks itself. Ready-prepared stocks are widely available now and many are tasty, but they tend to be expensive. Homemade stock is easy and economical. The ingredients for stock can vary enormously, and should reflect what you have available, with some consideration given to the eventual purpose of the stock. In addition to the bones of meat or poultry or fish, aromatic vegetables, such as carrot, onion and garlic, are essential. Other vegetables, like leeks or their greens, shallots, mushrooms, parsnips, celery or celeriac, may also be included. Keep

in mind that strongly flavored vegetables like cabbage, kale or turnips should be used with discretion and avoided in stocks destined for delicate soups.

Vegetarian stocks need more than just the usual aromatic vegetables to give them depth of flavor. Lettuce, cabbage, spinach or other greens, additional herbs and a substantial amount of the above vegetables should be used. Include some sweet ones, such as parsnips or celeriac, or a small apple or pear.

Unless you buy your meat at a butcher or a supermarket where meat is cut on the premises, it is not always easy to obtain meat bones for stock. Veal bones give more flavor than beef bones. Chicken bones are more readily available, and a rich brown chicken stock can be used in place of meat stock in most recipes.

It is best not to add salt to stock; it will be concentrated during evaporation or reduction. Season your soup, or whatever you are making, after adding stock.

Procedure

Use cold water in stock-making; it helps to extract impurities and enables the ingredients to yield their flavor. Remember that the water should be in proportion to the rest of the ingredients – in other words, don't drown them. The amount varies with the container used and the density of the ingredients in it, but for maximum flavor, keep the stock ingredients covered with about 1 inch of water, and top up with cold water if the level of the liquid falls below the solids.

When a richer flavor or deeper color is needed, brown the ingredients by roasting or sautéeing them before adding to the stockpot.

Skimming is vital. The scum or foam is impurities rising to the surface. If not removed, they will cook into the stock and it will be cloudy. Well skimmed, slowly "brewed" stock can be remarkably clear.

Cook stock uncovered, or partially covered, and avoid boiling it. Boiling clouds stock and causes fat to be emulsified or incorporated into the liquid; it is not then possible to remove it or its greasy taste. If the pot is covered, the stock is likely to boil no matter how low the heat under it, and it may sour. Meat stock needs 4–6 hours of simmering to extract all the goodness from the ingredients, but poultry stock only requires about half this time, up to 3 hours. Simmer fish stock for about 30 minutes; if cooked too long, it can acquire a bitter taste.

Strain through a fine-mesh strainer as soon as it is ready. For the most limpid stock, line the strainer with damp cheesecloth.

Remove the fat before using stock. Either chill to allow the fat to congeal on top and lift it off, or pour warm stock into a fat separator, or degreasing pitcher, let it stand until the fat rises to the top, then pour off the lean stock through the spout at the bottom. You can also spoon off the fat, but this is less effective.

If the taste of your stock is insipid, reduce it to concentrate the flavor. Soups in which stock is the major element must be rich in flavor. Reduction is also used to concentrate the volume for storage. If you want completely clear stock, as for consommé, it must always be clarified. Since the clarification process removes some of the stock's original flavor, other ingredients are added to fortify it, cut into small pieces to yield flavor quickly, but the clarification itself is actually accomplished by the addition of egg whites, usually one white per quart.

Fresh stock keeps for about 3 days, refrigerated, and it can be boiled again and stored for a further 2–3 days. It can be reduced to a glaze and refrigerated, or frozen in ice cube trays, so the cubes can then be added to soups and sauces to enrich the flavor without defrosting.

The shape of a stockpot permits the slow reduction of liquid, so it is as good for a long simmered meat stock as a quickly made seafood stock. Because the vegetables and other ingredients are densely packed, the proportion of water is usually right.

~.~.~.~.~.~.~.~.~.~.~

Stock-Making Tips

Save stock ingredients in the freezer as you accumulate them: poultry giblets, necks, backs and carcasses, scraps and cooked bones from roasts, trimmings and raw bones from poultry or meat you have boned yourself, clean vegetable trimmings such as leek greens, spring onion tops, mushroom stalks, celery leaves and pithy branches, slightly wilted herbs or the remaining half onions when you have chopped the other half.

Store in tightly sealed plastic freezer bags or boxes.

To improve the flavor of stock made from bouillon cubes or granules, add half again or twice the amount of water indicated in the instructions and simmer for about 30 minutes with aromatic vegetables and herbs. Canned chicken broth and beef consommé are useful to have on hand, but it also benefits from diluting with a little water and simmering with herbs if time permits.

~.~.~.~.~.~.~.~.~.~.~

Stock Recipes

*U*se the following stock recipes as a framework for stock-making. Make smaller or larger batches or vary the ingredients, if you wish, but be sure to use enough ingredients in your stock to give good flavor or it will need to be reduced to concentrate the flavor and some of the volume will be lost.

MEAT STOCK

A variety of ingredients may be used in making meat stock. Veal bones give more flavor than beef bones, but they are not easy to obtain. If the bones have no meat on them, it is best to add some stewing beef. You can also use a meaty cut such as shank or oxtail and add some chicken necks, backs or carcasses to provide gelatin. Avoid lamb bones unless you want to make lamb stock.

MAKES ABOUT 10 CUPS

6–7 pounds meaty bones and meat (including veal or beef knuckle, shank or other bones, oxtails, bones from roasts, poultry carcasses and/or poultry necks, giblets, etc)

2 large unpeeled onions, halved and root end trimmed

2 carrots, scrubbed and cut in large pieces

1 celery stalk, cut in large pieces

2 leeks, cut in large pieces

1–2 parsnips, cut in large pieces (optional)

2–4 unpeeled garlic cloves, lightly crushed

large bouquet garni (parsley stems, thyme sprigs, celery leaves and bay leaf)

3–4 cloves (optional)

6–8 allspice berries (optional)

❶ Put the bones and meat, the onions, carrots, celery, leeks, parsnips, if using, and garlic in a large stockpot or heavy saucepan, pushing the vegetables down between the bones. Cover with cold water by at least 2 inches and bring to a boil over medium-high heat. As the liquid heats, foam will begin to appear on the surface. As soon as it appears and until it stops surfacing, skim off the foam with a skimmer or perforated spoon.

❷ When the stock reaches boiling point, reduce the heat to low and add the *bouquet garni* and spices, if using. Simmer very slowly, uncovered, for about 4–5 hours, skimming occasionally and topping up with cold water if the liquid level falls below the solids. Gently ladle the stock through a strainer, lined with damp cheesecloth if you wish, into a large container.

❸ To remove the fat, chill the stock to allow it to congeal, then scrape off the fat. Gently remove any further traces of fat by wiping a paper towel lightly across the surface. If time is short, use a fat separator to remove the fat from the warm stock or spoon off the fat. Blot any remaining beads of fat with paper towels.

❹ If you wish, reduce the stock to concentrate the flavor. Store in the refrigerator or freezer.

Ham Stock
See Ham and Split Pea Soup, page 53.

BROWN STOCK

Put the bones, meat and vegetables in a large roasting tin and brown in a preheated 450°F oven for 30–40 minutes, turning occasionally. Transfer the ingredients to the stockpot, discarding the fat, and add the *bouquet garni*, cloves and allspice berries. Proceed as for Meat Stock.

CHICKEN STOCK

Chicken bones are more readily available than meat bones, so chicken stock is easier – as well as quicker – to make. If you want cooked chicken meat for your soup, or for another purpose, use a whole boiling fowl or roasting chicken.

MAKES ABOUT 8 CUPS

4–4½ pounds raw chicken backs, necks, or raw or cooked carcasses or whole or cut up chicken

2 large unpeeled onions, root end trimmed

3 carrots, scrubbed, cut in large pieces

1 celery stalk, cut in large pieces

1 leek, cut in large pieces

2 unpeeled garlic cloves, lightly crushed

large bouquet garni (parsley stems, thyme and marjoram or tarragon sprigs and bay leaf)

Proceed as for Meat Stock, but simmer for only 2–3 hours. If using a whole bird or pieces, cut off the breast meat after 25–30 minutes and return the remainder to the stockpot.

Variations

Brown Chicken Stock
Brown the chicken pieces in a frying pan over medium heat until golden and transfer to the stockpot, discarding the fat. Proceed as for Chicken Stock.

Turkey Stock
Remove any stuffing, break or chop the carcass into pieces and, if you wish, add sage leaves to the *bouquet garni*. Proceed as for Chicken Stock.

Game Stock
Proceed as for Chicken Stock, with or without initial browning.

FISH STOCK

Fish stock is quick and easy to make. The initial cooking of the fish parts in butter makes a richer stock, but if you wish, omit this step and combine all the ingredients in the stockpot. Avoid using the bones of oily fish, such as mackerel or salmon for all-purpose stock.

MAKES ABOUT 6 CUPS

1 tablespoon butter

2 pounds heads, bones and trimmings from fresh white fish

1 onion, thinly sliced

1 carrot, thinly sliced

1 leek, thinly sliced

1 cup dry white wine

5 cups water

6–8 parsley stems

6–8 black peppercorns

❶ Melt the butter in a large nonreactive saucepan or flameproof casserole over medium-high heat and add the fish parts. Cook for 2–3 minutes and add the vegetables, wine, water, parsley stems and peppercorns.

❷ Bring to a boil, skimming off any foam that rises to the top. Reduce the heat to low and simmer gently for 25 minutes. Ladle the stock through a strainer lined with cheesecloth and remove any fat.

SHELLFISH STOCK

Don't throw away the shells of crustaceans. Make this stock with the shells of shrimp, scampi or lobster you have enjoyed for another meal.

MAKES ABOUT 6 CUPS

½–1 pound shrimp, or lobster shells, heads and legs

1 onion, chopped

1 small carrot, sliced

1 celery stalk, sliced

½ lemon (unwaxed or scrubbed), thinly sliced

6 cups water

bouquet garni (parsley stems, thyme sprigs and leek greens)

❶ Combine the shellfish shells and parts with the vegetables, lemon, water and *bouquet garni* in a saucepan. Bring to a boil, skimming off any foam as it rises to the top.

❷ Reduce the heat to low and simmer gently, partially covered, for 25 minutes. Ladle the stock through a strainer lined with cheesecloth and remove any fat.

VEGETABLE STOCK

With vegetable stock, it is even more important to balance the proportion of water to ingredients and to give some thought to the eventual use of the stock so you can select suitable ingredients. Cut the vegetables more finely than for long-simmered stocks so that they can yield their goodness quickly and include plenty of other seasonal vegetables along with the basic ones.

MAKES ABOUT 8 CUPS

1 large onion, halved and thinly sliced
2 shallots, thinly sliced
2 carrots, thinly sliced
1 parsnip, thinly sliced
1 large leek, thinly sliced
1–2 turnips or ½ rutabaga, halved and thinly sliced
1 potato, cut in large chunks
2–3 ounces mushrooms or mushroom stems

2–3 ounces green beans or green bean trimmings (optional)
5–6 ounces cabbage, or 3–4 ounces other greens, such as lettuce, chard or kale
large bouquet garni (parsley stems, thyme and marjoram sprigs, a few rosemary or sage leaves and 1–2 bay leaves)

❶ Combine the ingredients in a large stockpot, add cold water to cover by at least 1 inch. Bring to a boil over medium-high heat, skimming off any foam as it rises to the top.
❷ Reduce the heat to low and simmer gently for about 45 minutes. Ladle the stock through a strainer lined with cheesecloth and remove any fat.

GARLIC STOCK

This herb and garlic infusion is a basic vegetable stock that you can make quickly with ingredients you are likely to have on hand.

MAKES ABOUT 6 CUPS

6 cups water
1 large garlic bulb (about 20 garlic cloves), unpeeled
4–6 thyme sprigs, or ½ teaspoon dried thyme

6 marjoram sprigs, or ½ teaspoon dried marjoram
bay leaf

❶ Combine the water, garlic, thyme, marjoram and bay leaf in a saucepan.
❷ Bring to a boil, reduce the heat to medium-low and simmer, partially covered, for 30–45 minutes then strain.

SPICED VEGETABLE STOCK

This Indian-spiced stock makes a good base for curried soups or stews.

MAKES ABOUT 6 CUPS

1 tablespoon vegetable oil
1 large onion, sliced
1 large leek, sliced
2 carrots, chopped
1 celery stick with leaves, sliced
2 garlic cloves, peeled and crushed
1 teaspoon coriander seeds
3 cardamom pods

2 cloves
½ teaspoon each cumin seed and mustard seed
½ teaspoon each dried thyme and oregano
6 cups water
6–8 parsley stems
½ lemon (unwaxed or scrubbed), thinly sliced

❶ Heat the oil in a large heavy saucepan or stockpot over medium heat. Add the onion, leek, carrots and celery, and cook until the onion becomes softer and slightly transparent. Add the spices and dried herbs, and continue cooking for 2–3 minutes.
❷ Stir in the water, parsley and lemon, and bring to a boil. Reduce the heat to low and simmer for 30–40 minutes. Strain the stock and remove any fat.

~·~·~·~·~·~·~·~·~·~·~

COOK'S TIP
The addition of spices can contribute to an interesting stock, but they should only be used when it is destined for a soup you know they will enhance. Otherwise wait and add spices to the soup itself.

~·~·~·~·~·~·~·~·~·~

CHAPTER ONE

Vegetable Soups

SOUP IS A PERFECT WAY TO CELEBRATE THE
ABUNDANT PROFUSION OF EACH VEGETABLE
AS THE GROWING SEASON PROGRESSES – FROM
SPRING ASPARAGUS TO FULL-BLOWN SUMMER
VEGETABLES SUCH AS TOMATOES, PEPPERS AND
EGGPLANT TO AUTUMN'S COLORFUL PUMPKINS
TO THE CHESTNUTS AND BEANS THAT WE
WELCOME IN WINTER. THE FOLLOWING RECIPES
OFFER EXCITING VEGETABLE SOUPS FOR EVERY
MONTH OF THE YEAR.

VEGETABLE SOUPS

*V*egetables provide limitless opportunity for soup-making. Their versatility makes them a logical choice, whether you want a light and refreshing purée of fresh greens, a thick creamy chowder or a robust tomato soup.

Many of these soups feature vegetables puréed to a smooth velvety consistency that puts the focus on their unique flavors. These usually have only one or two main ingredients, so the flavor is distinct. Often no additional thickening is used, as the vegetables themselves provide the needed bulk. A little cream is a pleasant addition, but this is always optional. Puréed soups have a certain formality that makes them perfect served as first courses, but they are equally satisfying at other times.

Compound soups, like Provençal Vegetable Soup or Tuscan Bean and Kale Soup, tend to be heartier but may be less rich. They contain a variety of ingredients which are eaten with their cooking

Almost any vegetable is good made into soup, whether a smooth purée, such as asparagus soup, or a chunky mixture, like vegetable chowder. Some vegetables are an asset to any soup – potato, for instance, is often added to thicken other soups.

liquid and such soups may be thick or thin, depending on the density of vegetables in them.

Leftovers can be the springboard for vegetable soups, as well as other kinds. Just bring your creativity and common sense to the task and give some thought to how flavors will combine. Start by cooking an onion in butter, with perhaps other aromatic vegetables, such as carrot and leek or garlic – just as most of the soups in this chapter begin. A straightforward recipe, like Sweet Potato and Leek Soup, can provide the basic procedure. Then you can substitute leftovers – for instance, mashed potatoes in place of the sweet and white potatoes in the recipe.

These soups can all be adapted to your own taste. A little more tomato, a little less cream, a little different seasoning may well be an improvement.

~.~.~.~.~.~.~.~.~.~.•

"Beautiful soup, so rich and green,
Waiting for a hot tureen,
Who for such dainties would not stoop?
Soup of the evening, beautiful soup!"

ALICE IN WONDERLAND
Lewis Carroll, 1832–98

~·~·~·~·~·~·~·~·~

PROVENCAL VEGETABLE SOUP

(Soupe au Pistou)

The *pistou*, a kind of Provençal *pesto* sauce which is stirred in at the end, gives this vegetable soup a special zing, so don't leave it out. The assortment of vegetables, however, can be varied according to availability.

SERVES 6

1½ cups (10 ounces) fresh shelled fava, coco or cranberry beans, or ¾ cup (6 ounces) dried beans, soaked overnight
¼ teaspoon dried herbes de Provence
2 garlic cloves, minced
1 tablespoon olive oil
1 medium onion, finely chopped
1 large leek, split and finely sliced
1 celery stick, finely sliced
2 thin carrots, finely diced
2 small potatoes, finely diced
4 ounces thin green beans
5 cups water

salt and freshly ground pepper
1 cup shelled peas, fresh or frozen
2 small zucchini, quartered lengthwise and finely sliced
3 medium tomatoes, peeled, seeded and finely chopped
a handful of spinach leaves, cut in thin ribbons

BASIL PUREE
1 large or 2 small garlic cloves, very finely chopped
½ cup (packed) basil leaves
4 tablespoons freshly grated Parmesan cheese
4 tablespoons extra-virgin olive oil

❶ To make the basil purée, put the garlic, basil and cheese in a food processor fitted with a steel blade and process until thoroughly puréed, scraping down the sides once. With the machine running, slowly pour the olive oil through the feed tube. Alternatively, pound the garlic, basil and cheese in a pestle and mortar, then slowly stir in the oil.

❷ Put the fresh or soaked beans in a large saucepan with the dried herbs and 1 of the garlic cloves, and add water to cover by 1 inch. Bring to a boil, reduce the heat and simmer over medium–low heat until the beans are cooked, about 20 minutes for fresh beans, or about 1 hour for dried beans. Set aside in the cooking liquid.

❸ Heat the olive oil in a large saucepan over medium-low heat. Add the onion and leek, and cook for 5 minutes, stirring occasionally, until the onion softens. Add the celery, carrots and the remaining garlic, and cook, covered, for another 10 minutes, stirring frequently.

❹ Add the potatoes, green beans and water. Season lightly with salt and pepper. Bring to a boil, reduce the heat to low and simmer, covered, for 10 minutes.

❺ Add the peas, zucchini and tomatoes. Add the cooked broad beans with the cooking liquid and simmer for 25–30 minutes, or until all the vegetables are tender. Taste for seasoning. Add the spinach and simmer for 5 minutes longer. Ladle into warm bowls and swirl a spoonful of basil purée into each.

TUSCAN WHITE BEAN *and* KALE SOUP

This soup is perfect for a fireside supper on a winter's evening. Serve it with warm *focaccio* or garlic bread.

SERVES 6

1¼ cups (8 ounces) dried borlotti or navy beans, soaked overnight in cold water to cover generously
1 tablespoon olive oil
3½ ounces pancetta or smoked lean bacon, chopped
1 onion, finely chopped
1 shallot, finely chopped
1 carrot, finely chopped
1–2 garlic cloves, minced
4 tomatoes, peeled, seeded and chopped, or

1¾ cups canned chopped tomatoes
5 cups water
bouquet garni (thyme and marjoram sprigs, parsley stems and bay leaf)
4 ounces curly kale leaves, finely chopped (2 lightly packed cups)
freshly grated or shaved Parmesan cheese, for serving (optional)

❶ Drain the beans, put into a saucepan with cold water to cover and set over high heat. Bring to a boil and boil for 10 minutes. Drain and add fresh cold water to cover. Bring to a boil again, drain and rinse well.

❷ Heat the oil in a large heavy saucepan over medium-high heat and add the pancetta or bacon. Cook until lightly browned, stirring frequently. Remove with a slotted spoon to drain on paper towels and pour off all but 1 tablespoon of the fat. Reduce the heat to low, add the onion, shallot, carrot and garlic, and cook for 3–4 minutes until slightly softened. Add the beans, tomatoes, water, *bouquet garni* and pancetta or bacon, and simmer until the beans are tender, 1–2 hours. Season to taste with salt and pepper.

❸ Stir in the kale and continue cooking for 15–20 minutes, or until it is tender. Adjust the seasoning and ladle the soup into warm bowls. Serve sprinkled with Parmesan cheese, if you wish.

~.~.~.~.~.~.~.~.~

TO DRINK
A medium-dry red wine, such as Côtes de Provence or Navarra.

~.~.~.~.~.~.~.~.~

EMERALD SOUP

In this gloriously colored soup, the sharpness of the watercress is tamed by the pear. It is pretty served in glass bowls.

SERVES 4

1 tablespoon butter
1 large onion, chopped
1 small potato, diced
4 cups chicken stock
bouquet garni (1 sprig each
 fresh marjoram and thyme
 and 1 bay leaf)
1 large ripe pear, cored, peeled
 and chopped

1 bunch watercress, washed
 and stems discarded, about
 1½ cups packed leaves
1 pound young spinach, washed
 and stems discarded
salt and freshly ground pepper
freshly ground nutmeg
watercress sprigs, for
 garnishing

❶ Melt the butter in a heavy saucepan over medium heat. Add the onion and cook until golden, 3–4 minutes. Add the potato, stock and *bouquet garni*. Cook gently until the vegetables are tender, about 25 minutes.

❷ Stir in the pear and cook for 2 minutes. Remove the *bouquet garni*. Add the watercress and spinach, and continue cooking for 3–4 minutes, stirring frequently until the leaves are completely wilted.

❸ Transfer the soup to a blender or a food processor fitted with a steel blade and purée until smooth, working in batches if necessary. Return to the saucepan and season to taste with salt, pepper and nutmeg. Set the pan over medium-low heat and simmer for 4–5 minutes until reheated. Ladle the soup into warm bowls or soup plates and garnish with watercress sprigs.

JERUSALEM ARTICHOKE SOUP

This native North American vegetable was introduced in England from Massachusetts. It became a favorite of the Victorians and this silky, genteel soup is typical.

SERVES 3–4

1 lemon (unwaxed or scrubbed)
1 pound Jerusalem artichokes
1 tablespoon butter
1 shallot, chopped
½ onion, chopped
3 cups white chicken or veal
 stock

3 tablespoons whipping
 cream
salt and white pepper
borage flowers or flat-leaf
 parsley, for garnishing

❶ Finely grate the zest from the lemon and set aside. Fill a bowl with cold water and add the juice of ½ lemon.

❷ Peel the Jerusalem artichokes and cut large ones in two or three pieces. Drop into the acidulated water to prevent discoloration.

❸ Melt the butter in a heavy saucepan over medium heat. Add the shallot and onion and cook, stirring frequently, until just softened, about 4 minutes. Drain the Jerusalem artichokes and add them to the pan with the stock. Bring just to a boil, reduce the heat to medium-low and simmer gently until the vegetables are tender, 15–20 minutes.

❹ Transfer the solids to a blender or a food processor fitted with a steel blade, add some of the cooking liquid and purée until smooth. Return to the saucepan with the remaining cooking liquid, add the cream, salt, pepper and lemon zest and juice to taste. Set over medium-low heat and simmer for 3–5 minutes until reheated. Ladle the soup into warm bowls and float a borage flower or parsley leaf on top.

EGGPLANT *and* RED PEPPER SOUP

Roasting the eggplants before making the soup gives a rich, mellow flavor. If you wish, you can roast the vegetables up to 2 days ahead. Refrigerate them, wrapped, until needed.

SERVES 4–6

2 large eggplants	*4 cups chicken stock*
2 large red bell peppers	*pinch of dried thyme*
Tabasco sauce	*5–6 coriander seeds*
1½ tablespoons olive oil	*1 teaspoon tomato paste*
1 large onion, finely chopped	*6 tablespoons whipping cream*
3 garlic cloves, finely chopped	*salt and pepper*

❶ Preheat the oven to 400°F. Place the eggplants and peppers in a shallow roasting pan and roast until the pepper skins are evenly darkened, about 1 hour, turning the vegetables three or four times. Put the peppers in a sturdy plastic bag, seal tightly and allow to steam.

❷ When the vegetables are cool enough to handle, peel the eggplants and cut into cubes. Working over a bowl to catch the liquid, peel the skin from the peppers and remove the cores and seeds. Put the pepper flesh in a food processor fitted with a steel blade and strain in the liquid. Purée until smooth and season with Tabasco. Scrape into a small bowl and set aside.

❸ Heat the oil in a large heavy saucepan over medium-low heat. Add the onion and cook for 4–5 minutes, stirring frequently, until just softened. Add the garlic and continue cooking for 1 minute longer. Add the eggplant cubes, stock, thyme, coriander seeds and tomato paste. Cover and simmer for 30 minutes, or until the vegetables are very tender.

❹ Transfer the solids to a blender or a food processor fitted with a steel blade. Add some of the cooking liquid and purée until smooth, working in batches if necessary. Return the purée to the saucepan with the remaining cooking liquid, stir in the cream and adjust the seasoning, if necessary. Reheat the soup over medium-low heat for about 5 minutes, or until heated through. Ladle into warm bowls and top each serving with a dollop of the red pepper purée, dividing it evenly.

~.~.~.~.~.~.~.~.~.~

TO DRINK
A medium-bodied
fruity red wine, such
as Pinotage or
Beaujolais.

~.~.~.~.~.~.~.~.~.~

PUMPKIN *and* COCONUT SOUP

Served from a hollowed-out pumpkin, this spicy soup makes a dramatic and tasty starter. It is best to use another pumpkin for serving, as it is difficult to carve the flesh from the inside without piercing the shell. Cut enough from the top to make a wide opening – like a bowl – and scrape out the seeds and filaments. Warm the pumpkin shell in a slow oven or fill with boiling water and empty before filling with soup. Of course, the soup can be ladled into a warm tureen or individual bowls.

SERVES 6

milk from 1 coconut
1 tablespoon butter
1 large onion, chopped
1 large potato, cubed
2 garlic cloves, minced
1¾ pounds pumpkin, cubed
1 cup grated fresh coconut
1½ tablespoons finely chopped
   fresh gingerroot
¼ teaspoon crushed red pepper
   flakes

grated nutmeg
bouquet garni (thyme sprigs,
   parsley stems, lemon grass
   and bay leaf)
¾ cup whipping cream
6 tablespoons coconut cream
salt and freshly ground pepper
toasted coconut strips, for
   garnishing

❶ Empty the coconut milk through a fine-mesh strainer lined with damp cheesecloth into a large measuring container. Add water to make 5 cups.
❷ Melt the butter in a large heavy saucepan over medium-low heat, add the onion and cook until just softened, about 4 minutes.
❸ Add the potato, garlic, pumpkin and the diluted coconut milk to the saucepan and bring to a boil. Reduce the heat to medium-low and add the grated coconut, gingerroot, red pepper flakes, a generous grating of nutmeg and the *bouquet garni*. Simmer, stirring occasionally, until the vegetables are very tender, 15–20 minutes.
❹ Remove the *bouquet garni* and transfer the solids to a blender or a food processor fitted with a steel blade. Add some of the cooking liquid and purée until smooth, working in batches if necessary. Return the purée to the pan with the remaining liquid and stir in the cream. Season to taste with salt and pepper.
❺ Reheat the soup gently over low heat. Pour or ladle the soup into a warm pumpkin shell, or a tureen or bowls, and sprinkle with toasted coconut strips.

~.~.~.~.~.~.~.~.~.~

COOK'S TIP
To make toasted coconut
strips, remove all the bark and
skin and cut pieces of coconut
into paper-thin slices about
2 inches long. Spread the slices
on a baking sheet and toast in a
preheated 325°F oven until
lightly browned.
Sprinkle with salt,
if you wish.

~.~.~.~.~.~.~.~.~.~

GARDEN VEGETABLE CHOWDER

The crispy onion garnish gives a pleasant contrast to the creaminess of the soup, but it is equally good topped with grated Cheddar cheese.

SERVES 6–8

2 tablespoons butter
1 onion, chopped
1 shallot, chopped
1 leek, split lengthwise and thinly sliced
1–2 garlic cloves, minced
3 tablespoons flour
3 carrots, halved lengthwise and thinly sliced
½ small celeriac, finely diced, or 2 celery stalks, finely sliced
2 small turnips, finely diced

2 large baking potatoes, diced
3 cups vegetable or light chicken stock
bouquet garni (thyme and marjoram sprigs, parsley stems and bay leaf)
salt and white pepper
1 cup chopped green beans
kernels cut from 2 ears of corn
1⅓ cups milk
¾ cup whipping cream
crispy fried onions (see page 124)

❶ Melt the butter in a large heavy saucepan over medium heat. Add the onion, shallot, leek, and garlic. Cook until the vegetables start to soften, about 5 minutes, stirring frequently. Stir in the flour and cook for 2 minutes. Add the carrots, celeriac or celery, turnips, potatoes and stock, stirring and scraping the bottom of the pan.

❷ Bring to a boil, stirring frequently. Add the *bouquet garni* and season with salt and pepper. Reduce the heat to medium-low and simmer, stirring occasionally, until the vegetables are almost tender, about 20 minutes.

❸ Stir in the beans, corn and milk. Continue cooking until the beans are tender, about 10 minutes. Stir in the cream, adjust the seasoning and heat through. Remove the *bouquet garni*. Ladle into warm bowls and garnish with crispy fried onions.

WILD MUSHROOM SOUP

This soup gets a flavor boost from the minced mushroom base, or *duxelles*, one of the basic building blocks of French cooking. If wild mushrooms are not available, use the most flavorful domestic mushrooms you can find.

SERVES 4

8 ounces wild mushrooms or cultivated wild varieties (porcini, chanterelles, oyster or shiitake), wiped or rinsed and blotted dry
1 pound button mushrooms, wiped or rinsed and blotted dry
2 tablespoons butter
2 shallots, finely chopped
1 garlic clove, chopped
salt and freshly ground pepper

6 cups beef or brown chicken stock
2 tablespoons flour
2–3 tablespoons Cognac or brandy
bouquet garni (thyme and marjoram sprigs, parsley stems and bay leaf)
freshly grated nutmeg
½ cup whipping cream
chopped fresh chives, for garnishing

❶ Cut the stems of the wild mushrooms level with the caps. Thinly slice the wild mushroom caps and set aside, and put the stems in a food processor fitted with a steel blade. Add the button mushrooms to the processor and pulse until finely chopped. (They should look like fine breadcrumbs.)

❷ Melt half the butter in a nonstick frying pan over medium heat and cook the shallots until just softened, 2–3 minutes. Add the chopped mushrooms and garlic. Continue cooking, stirring frequently, until the mushrooms have rendered and re-absorbed their liquid and are almost completely dry and starting to brown, about 10 minutes. Season with salt and pepper. Transfer to a blender, add a quarter of the stock and blend until smooth. (Blending improves the texture, but can be omitted.)

❸ Melt the remaining butter in a saucepan over medium heat, add the wild mushroom caps and cook for 4–5 minutes, or until they are lightly browned. Sprinkle over the flour and cook for 2–3 minutes, stirring frequently, until well blended.

❹ Stir in the Cognac and remaining stock. Add the *bouquet garni*, nutmeg and the blended mushroom and stock mixture. Simmer, covered, over low heat for 20–30 minutes, stirring occasionally.

❺ Just before serving, remove the *bouquet garni*, stir in the cream and cook for 1–2 minutes to heat through. Ladle into a warm tureen or soup bowls and sprinkle with chives.

SWEET POTATO *and* LEEK SOUP

This soup is wonderfully smooth and creamy with an elusive flavor that is hard to identify. If you are able to find sweet potatoes with pale yellow flesh and a consistency more like white potatoes than yams, omit the white potato from this recipe.

SERVES 6

1 tablespoon butter	*salt and freshly ground pepper*
4 medium leeks (about 12 ounces), thinly sliced	*freshly grated nutmeg*
2½ cups chicken stock
1¾ pounds sweet potatoes, peeled and cubed	*⅔ cup whipping cream*
3 tablespoons finely chopped fresh chives
1 medium white potato, cubed	
4 cups water	

❶ Melt the butter in a large, heavy saucepan over medium-low heat. Add the leeks, cover and cook for 6–8 minutes, or until softened.

❷ Add the sweet potatoes, white potato and water. Season lightly with salt, pepper and nutmeg. Bring to a boil over high heat. Reduce the heat to medium-low and simmer, partially covered, for about 20 minutes until the vegetables are very tender, stirring occasionally.

❸ Transfer the vegetables and cooking liquid to a blender or a food processor fitted with a steel blade and purée until smooth, working in batches if necessary. Strain the mixture back into the saucepan, pressing firmly with the back of a spoon to extract as much liquid as possible. Stir in the stock, set over low heat and simmer for 10–15 minutes, or until heated through. Taste and adjust the seasoning.

❹ Using an electric mixer or whisk, whip the cream with a pinch of salt until soft peaks form. Stir in the chives.

❺ Ladle the soup into warm bowls or soup plates and garnish with the chive-flavored whipped cream.

CORN CHOWDER

Both corn and potatoes originated in South America and found their way to other parts of the world via North America. Dried corn was used for this soup in the days before modern agriculture and transportation ensured the availability of fresh corn all year. This recipe is quite rich; if you prefer, use more milk instead of the cream.

SERVES 4–6

1 tablespoon butter	*3 cups water*
3 ounces thick-cut lean smoked back bacon, finely chopped	*salt and freshly ground pepper*
4 ears corn
1 onion, finely chopped	*¾ cup whipping cream*
1 pound potatoes, diced	*½ cup milk*

❶ Melt the butter in a large heavy saucepan over medium-high heat. Add the bacon and onion, and cook, stirring frequently, until the onion is soft and the bacon golden, about 7 minutes.

❷ Add the potatoes and water, and season lightly with salt and pepper. Reduce the heat to medium-low and simmer, partially covered, until the potatoes are just tender, about 15 minutes.

❸ Cut the kernels from the corn, without cutting down to the cob. With the back of a knife, scrape the cobs to extract the milky liquid from the base of kernels. Alternatively, use a corn scraper to remove the kernels and the liquid in one process.

❹ Add the corn and its liquid to the saucepan with the cream and continue cooking for about 10 minutes, until all the vegetables are tender. Stir in the milk, adding more if needed to thin the soup to the preferred consistency. Simmer for 2–3 minutes until heated through. Taste and adjust the seasoning and ladle into a warm tureen or bowls.

CARAMELIZED ONION SOUP *with* CORNMEAL FRITTERS

This rich satisfying soup is a variation on the classic French onion soup, which is served with a croûton covered with grated cheese and toasted until brown and bubbly. These small cornmeal fritters are lighter and make an unusual garnish.

SERVES 4

1 tablespoon butter	CORNMEAL FRITTERS
1½ tablespoons olive oil	*¾ cup water*
1½ pounds large yellow	*1 egg*
* onions, thinly sliced*	*⅔ cup cornmeal*
1 garlic clove, finely chopped	*salt and freshly ground pepper*
¼ teaspoon sugar	*6 tablespoons freshly grated*
salt	* Parmesan cheese*
2 tablespoons flour	*1 tablespoon finely chopped*
⅔ cup dry white wine	* chives or spring onion tops*
5 cups beef stock	*oil, for frying*

❶ In a large heavy saucepan or flameproof casserole, melt the butter and olive oil over medium-low heat. Add the onions and cook, covered, for 10–12 minutes until they soften, stirring occasionally. Add the garlic, sugar and a pinch of salt, and continue cooking, uncovered, for 45–55 minutes, or until the onions turn a deep, golden brown, stirring occasionally until they start to color, then more frequently.

❷ Stir in the flour until it is absorbed and cook for 2 minutes. Add the wine and a quarter of the stock, and bring to a boil, scraping the bottom of the pan and stirring until smooth. Add the remaining stock, reduce the heat to medium-low and simmer gently, partially covered, for 30 minutes.

❸ For the fritters, preheat the oven to 400°F. Put the water in a small bowl and beat in the egg. Slowly whisk in the cornmeal until smoothly blended. Season generously with salt and pepper, and stir in half the cheese and the chives. Set a large frying pan over medium-high heat and add enough oil to film the bottom of the pan. When it starts to smoke, drop the batter by scant tablespoonfuls, stirring it frequently. Cook the fritters until bubbles appear at the edges, about 1–1½ minutes, then turn over and cook for about 1 minute longer until evenly browned. Drain on paper towels and continue cooking in batches. Place the fritters on a baking sheet and sprinkle with the remaining cheese.

Bake at the top of the oven until the cheese is melted.

❹ Ladle the hot soup into warm bowls or soup plates and garnish each with three or four fritters.

~.~.~.~.~.~.~.~.~.~

TO DRINK
A young but
full-bodied red wine,
such as Côtes-du-
Rhone from France
or Dâo from Portugal.

~.~.~.~.~.~.~.~.~.~

SPICY BLACK BEAN SOUP

This soup has its roots in Cuba, but it shows the influence of contemporary chefs and the excitement of the food scene in Florida today.

SERVES 4–6

2½ cups (1 pound) black beans
1 tablespoon olive oil
2 red onions, finely chopped
4 garlic cloves, minced
5 tablespoons brandy
8 cups water
bouquet garni (bay leaf, thyme and marjoram sprigs, coriander and parsley stems and 2–3 strips orange zest)
½ teaspoon cumin seeds
¼ teaspoon dried oregano

3–4 roasted ancho chilli peppers, seeded and chopped, or ¼ teaspoon crushed dried chilies
1 tablespoon tomato paste
3 tomatoes, peeled, seeded and chopped
salt and freshly ground pepper
6 tablespoons sour cream
3–4 spring onions, finely chopped
cilantro leaves, for garnishing

❶ Pick over the beans to remove any small stones. Cover with cold water and leave to soak for 6 hours or overnight.
❷ Drain the beans, put into a saucepan with cold water to cover and set over high heat. Bring to a boil and boil for 10 minutes. Drain and rinse well.
❸ Heat the oil in a large, heavy saucepan over medium-high heat, add the onions and cook until they are just softened, 3–4 minutes, stirring frequently. Add the garlic and continue cooking for 2 minutes. Add the brandy, water, *bouquet garni*, cumin seeds, oregano and chillies. When the mixture begins to bubble, stir in the tomato paste, reduce the heat to low and simmer gently, partially covered, for 1½–2½ hours until the beans are tender, stirring occasionally. Remove and discard the *bouquet garni* and season with salt and, if you wish, pepper.
❹ Ladle the soup into a warm tureen or bowls and top with a dollop of sour cream. Sprinkle with the spring onions and garnish with cilantro.

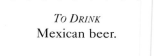

To Drink
Mexican beer.

CREAM *of* ASPARAGUS SOUP

The best asparagus for soup has large stalks and tightly closed tips. At the end of the season you can often find large quantities available at reasonable prices – a good time to make this soup.

SERVES 6–8

3 pounds fresh asparagus,
 woody ends removed
2 tablespoons butter
1 small onion, chopped
6 cups chicken stock
salt and freshly ground pepper

½ cup whipping cream
2 tablespoons cornstarch,
 blended with 3 tablespoons
 cold water
nasturtium flowers or shavings
 of Parmesan cheese,
 for garnishing

❶ Cut the asparagus into 1-inch pieces. Melt the butter in a large heavy saucepan over medium-high heat. Add the onion and the asparagus pieces, and cook for 5–6 minutes, stirring frequently, until the asparagus turns bright green (do not allow the pieces to brown).

❷ Stir in the stock and bring to a boil over high heat, skimming off any foam as it rises to the surface. Reduce the heat to medium and simmer for about 5 minutes until the tips are just tender. Using a slotted spoon, remove 12–16 asparagus tips for garnish. Set aside, covered. Season the soup with salt and pepper, cover and continue cooking for 15–20 minutes until the asparagus stalks are very tender.

❸ Transfer the vegetables and some of the cooking liquid to a blender or a food processor fitted with a steel blade and purée until smooth, working in batches if necessary. Strain the mixture back into the saucepan, pressing firmly with the back of a spoon to extract as much liquid as possible. Bring back to a boil over medium-high heat and stir in the cream. Stir the cornstarch mixture, whisk into the boiling soup and boil for 1–2 minutes until slightly thickened. Taste and adjust the seasoning.

❹ Ladle the soup into warm bowls and garnish with the reserved asparagus tips and nasturtium flowers or Parmesan shavings.

~.~.~.~.~.~.~.~.~

To Drink
A fresh, fruity
Chardonnay or Pinot
Grigio.

~.~.~.~.~.~.~.~.~

CHESTNUT *and* APPLE SOUP

This autumnal soup captures the flavors of the harvest – perfect as a starter at Christmas. For a more exotic, spicy soup, replace the sage with a cinnamon stick.

SERVES 4–6

1 pound shelled, skinned chestnuts
2 tablespoons butter
1 large onion, chopped
2 medium carrots, thinly sliced
2 medium dessert apples, peeled, cored and finely chopped
4 cups water

bouquet garni (bay leaf, 2 sage leaves, thyme sprigs and parsley stems)
salt and freshly ground pepper
4 tablespoons light cream, or as needed
sage leaves and chives, for garnishing

❶ Put the chestnuts in a saucepan, add water to cover and simmer over medium heat until chestnuts are just tender, 12–15 minutes. Remove from the heat and set aside.

❷ Melt the butter in a large heavy saucepan over medium-high heat, add the onion and carrots, and cook until the onion is just softened, about 5 minutes, stirring frequently. Add the apples, water, *bouquet garni* and chestnuts with their cooking liquid. Season with salt and pepper, and bring to a boil. Reduce the heat and simmer until all the vegetables are tender, about 25 minutes. Remove the *bouquet garni*.

❸ Transfer the solids to a blender or a food processor fitted with a metal blade, add some of the liquid and purée until smooth. Return to the saucepan, add the cream and simmer over low heat for a few minutes until heated through. Taste and adjust the seasoning. Ladle into a warm tureen or soup plates. If you like, garnish with sage leaves and chives on the edge of the plates.

~.~.~.~.~.~.~.~.~.~

To Drink
Sweet apple cider or sparkling dry hard cider, or an oaky Chardonnay.

Cook's Tip
To shell and skin chestnuts, use a small sharp knife to cut an "X" in the bottom of each chestnut. Bring a saucepan of water to the boil, add the chestnuts and boil for 6–8 minutes. Remove a few chestnuts at a time with a slotted spoon. Holding them in a towel or wearing rubber gloves, remove the shell with the aid of a paring knife, then peel off the inner skin.

~.~.~.~.~.~.~.~.~.~

CHEESE *and* CELERY BISQUE

This smooth soup makes a rich but light beginning to any number of menus. The recipe calls for Cheddar cheese, but try Stilton instead for a change of pace, especially during the holiday season.

SERVES 4

2 tablespoons butter
1 large carrot, finely chopped
4 large celery stalks, finely chopped
1 medium onion, finely chopped
4 cups chicken stock
bouquet garni (thyme and marjoram sprigs, parsley

stems and bay leaf)
½ cup whipping cream
1½ cups grated Cheddar cheese
salt (if needed) and freshly ground pepper
freshly grated nutmeg
celery leaves, for garnishing

❶ Melt the butter in a heavy saucepan over medium-high heat. Add the carrot, celery and onion, and cook, stirring occasionally, until the vegetables are slightly softened, about 5 minutes. Add the stock, bring to a boil, reduce the heat to low and simmer for 30 minutes.

❷ Strain the soup, pressing firmly with the back of a spoon to extract as much liquid as possible. Discard the solids and return the soup to the pan. Stir in the cream, set over low heat and simmer for 5 minutes. Slowly add the cheese, stirring constantly until smooth. Taste and adjust the seasoning, adding salt only if needed, and pepper to taste. (Do not allow the soup to boil.)

❸ Ladle into warm serving bowls or soup plates, grate a little nutmeg over each and garnish with celery leaves.

~.~.~.~.~.~.~.~.~

VARIATION
If preferred, substitute
5 ounces Stilton cheese,
grated, for the Cheddar.

TO DRINK
Lightly chilled
Tawny Port.

~.~.~.~.~.~.~.~.~

CELERIAC *and* FENNEL SOUP

This combination of winter vegetables has a fresh, intriguing, slightly sweet flavor that is difficult to identify.

SERVES 4–6

1 tablespoon butter
1 leek, split lengthwise and thinly sliced
1 small onion, chopped
1 small fennel bulb, chopped
1 large celeriac (about 1¾ pounds), peeled and cubed
1 medium potato, cubed

6 cups water
salt and white pepper
bouquet garni (2–3 sprigs thyme and/or marjoram and 1 bay leaf)
¾ cup milk, or more if needed
freshly grated nutmeg
fennel fronds, for garnishing

❶ Melt the butter in a large heavy saucepan over medium heat. Add the leek, onion and fennel, and cook, stirring frequently, until just softened, about 4 minutes. Add the celeriac, potato and water. Season with a little salt and add the *bouquet garni*. Bring to a boil over medium heat and boil gently until the vegetables are very tender, about 45 minutes.

❷ Remove the *bouquet garni* and transfer the solids to a blender or a food processor fitted with a steel blade. Add some of the cooking liquid and purée until smooth, working in batches if necessary.

❸ Return to the saucepan and stir in the milk, adding more if needed to thin the soup to the preferred consistency. Season to taste with salt, pepper and nutmeg. Reheat gently over low heat. Ladle into warm bowls and garnish with fennel fronds.

~.~.~.~.~.~.~.~.~

TO DRINK
Dry Oloroso sherry.

~.~.~.~.~.~.~.~.~

WILD RICE *and* WILD MUSHROOM CHOWDER

The dried mushrooms intensify the earthy flavor of the wild rice in this soup. Wild rice, which is actually an aquatic grass, is indigenous to North America and is still harvested by the native peoples of the US and Canada.

SERVES 4–6

2 ounces dried wild mushrooms
   (chanterelles or porcinis),
   rinsed if sandy
2 cups hot water
4 cups chicken stock
1 cup wild rice, rinsed in cold
   running water and drained
bouquet garni (thyme sprigs,
parsley stems and bay leaf)
2 tablespoons butter
2 shallots, finely chopped
3 tablespoons Cognac or dry
   sherry
salt and freshly ground pepper
6 tablespoons whipping cream
1 tablespoon finely chopped
   fresh thyme leaves

❶ Put the dried mushrooms in a bowl, add the water and leave to soak for 10 minutes. Strain the mushroom liquid through a strainer lined with damp cheesecloth into a saucepan. Squeeze or press the liquid from the mushrooms and reserve them. Add the stock, wild rice and *bouquet garni* to the mushroom liquid. Bring to a boil, reduce the heat to medium-low and simmer, partially covered, until the rice is soft and has completely split open, about 1½ hours.

❷ Strain the rice over a large bowl and discard the *bouquet garni*. Put the rice in a blender or a food processor fitted with a steel blade, add about a quarter of the cooking liquid and purée until smooth.

❸ Chop the mushrooms finely. Melt the butter in a large saucepan over medium-high heat. Add the shallots and mushrooms and cook until the shallots are soft and starting to color, 5–7 minutes. Stir in the remaining cooking liquid, Cognac or sherry and puréed rice. Season to taste with salt and pepper, and, if you wish, thin the soup with a little more stock or water. Bring to a boil, reduce the heat to low and simmer for about 5 minutes, or until heated through.

❹ Combine the cream and thyme in a small saucepan and set over low heat until bubbles appear around the edge. Ladle the soup into warm bowls or soup plates and swirl in the cream, dividing it evenly.

SESAME CARROT *and* PARSNIP SOUP

The subtle Oriental overtones in this soup elevate it from ordinary to exciting.

SERVES 4–6

1 tablespoon butter	salt and freshly ground pepper
1 onion, chopped	zest of ½ orange (unwaxed or
1 leek, split and sliced	scrubbed)
1 pound carrots, sliced	¼ teaspoon Oriental sesame oil,
2 medium parsnips, peeled and	or to taste
sliced	3 cups chicken or vegetable
1–2 garlic cloves, minced	stock
3 cups water	SESAME CROUTONS
7–8 coriander seeds	3 thin slices white or wholemeal
1–2 cardamom pods	bread, crusts removed
½ teaspoon fresh thyme leaves,	soft butter, for spreading
or a pinch of dried thyme	2 tablespoons sesame seeds

❶ Melt the butter in a large saucepan over medium heat and add the onion and leek. Cook until just softened, about 5 minutes, stirring occasionally. Add the carrots, parsnips, garlic and water. Tie the spices and thyme in a piece of cheesecloth and add to the soup with a little salt and pepper. Bring to a boil, reduce the heat to low and simmer gently, partially covered, until the vegetables are tender, about 45 minutes.

❷ Transfer the vegetables and cooking liquid to a blender or a food processor fitted with a steel blade and purée until smooth. Return to the saucepan, add the orange zest, sesame oil and stock, and simmer over very low heat, stirring occasionally.

❸ For the croutons, preheat the oven to 375°F. Spread the bread lightly with butter, sprinkle with sesame seeds and lightly press them into the butter to help them to adhere. Cut each piece of bread diagonally into four triangles, then cut each triangle in half to form two smaller triangles. Place them on a baking sheet and bake until pale golden and crispy, about 15 minutes.

❹ Ladle the soup into warm soup plates and top with croutons, dividing them evenly.

ROASTED TOMATO SOUP *with* GOAT'S CHEESE CROUTONS

Roasting the tomatoes and other vegetables gives this soup added flavor, essential if using winter tomatoes.

SERVES 4

2 garlic cloves, finely chopped	GOAT'S CHEESE CROUTONS
¼ teaspoon each dried thyme	4 slices French bread
and marjoram	3 ounces firm goat's cheese
3–4 tablespoons olive oil	(slightly smaller in diameter
2 pounds ripe tomatoes, cored	than the bread), cut in
and thickly sliced	4 slices
1 medium onion, chopped	
salt and freshly ground pepper	
1¼ cups vegetable or poultry	
stock	

❶ Preheat the oven to 375°. Mix together the garlic and herbs. Drizzle a tablespoonful of the olive oil in the bottom of a large shallow baking dish. Layer the tomatoes, onions and garlic-herb mixture in two or three layers. Drizzle each layer as you go with the olive oil and season with a little salt and pepper. Bake, uncovered, for 25 minutes, or until all the vegetables are soft.

❷ Work the vegetables through a food mill fitted with a fine blade set over a saucepan. Skim off any standing oil. Add the stock or water and simmer over medium heat, stirring occasionally, for about 15 minutes, or until heated through. Taste and adjust the seasoning, if necessary.

❸ For the goat's cheese croutons, preheat the broiler. Toast the bread lightly on both sides under the broiler. Top with slices of goat's cheese and broil until lightly browned.

❹ Ladle the soup into warm shallow bowls and place a crouton in each.

~.~.~.~.~.~.~.~.~.~.~

TO DRINK
A fruity red wine,
such as Beaujolais or
other Gamay wine.

~˙~˙~˙~˙~˙~˙~˙~˙~˙~

CHAPTER TWO

Meat Soups

Meat soups evoke some of our most beloved culinary traditions — the cauldron suspended in the chimney over glowing logs, the stockpot simmering on the back of the wood-fired stove. Rich aromas wafting through the air stir our senses and rekindle our appetite for one of man's favorite foods through the ages. Whether a light, elegant broth or a sustaining meal in a bowl, soup warms the heart as well as the stomach.

MEAT SOUPS

Nourishing meat soups are found in many cuisines around the world from the Far East to the Middle East to Europe to the Americas. Slow cooking is the common theme and cooking meat in liquid is one of the best ways to tenderize it. Long-simmered soups and stews produce a very rich broth. Pot au feu, *one of the cornerstones of French home cooking, is the classic example, but it has its counterparts in most other countries.*

Meat soups are often economical, as inexpensive cuts respond best to this treatment and also have more flavor. They usually contain other ingredients, such as vegetables, which give them more substance and stretch them, so a little meat goes a long way.

Leftover meat can be used to good advantage in some soups. Substitute it in recipes in which there are plenty of other ingredients to flavor the liquid, such as tomatoes or vegetables, and add any juices or gravy.

Stock made using bones benefits from long simmering to extract the gelatine from the bones, but soups and stocks made with boneless meat are faster. Cut the meat and vegetables into small pieces so they can yield their goodness and flavor quickly.

~.~.~.~.~.~.~.~.~.~.~

*"Meaty jelly, too, especially when a
little salt, which is the case when there's
ham, is mellering to the organ."*

OUR MUTUAL FRIEND
Charles Dickens, 1812–70

~.~.~.~.~.~.~.~.~.~.~

*Meat stock takes longer to make than other stocks because slow
simmering is needed to extract the gelatine from the bones and
develop a rich flavor, but you can make large batches and store it
in the freezer. An acceptable short-cut stock, taking only an hour,
can be made without bones by using finely chopped vegetables and
meat. Some of the following recipes use this technique, making the
stock and the soup at the same time.*

*The soups in this selection offer much variety. Some are light and
elegant, like Vintner's Oxtail Soup or Poached Beef and Vegetable
Soup, some rich and aromatic, such as Italian Sausage and
Zucchini Soup, some thick and satisfying, for instance, Arab Lamb
and Chick-pea Soup or Texas Chili.*

ARAB LAMB *and* CHICK-PEA SOUP

(Harira)

Redolent of exotic Middle Eastern spices, this soup, a slightly tamed version of the Moroccan mutton soup *harira*, is satisfying and unusual. Lentils, dried beans or pasta are sometimes added for an even more substantial soup and in Morocco, dates are offered as an accompaniment.

SERVES 4–6

¾ cup chick-peas (garbanzos), soaked overnight and drained, or 1¾ cups canned chick-peas, rinsed and drained
1½–2 tablespoons olive oil
1½ pounds boneless lamb shoulder, trimmed of all fat and cut into 1-inch cubes
1 onion, finely chopped
3 garlic cloves, minced
4 tablespoons dry white wine (optional)
5 cups water
¾ teaspoon dried thyme
¾ teaspoon dried oregano
bay leaf
¼ teaspoon ground cinnamon
¼ teaspoon cumin seeds

4 tomatoes, peeled, seeded and chopped, or 1 cup tomato juice
2 roasted red bell peppers, peeled, seeded and chopped
¼ teaspoon ground saffron or turmeric
1 large leek, halved lengthwise and sliced
1 large carrot, diced
1 large potato, diced
2 medium zucchini, halved lengthwise and sliced
⅔ cup fresh or thawed frozen green peas
harissa (hot red pepper paste), to taste
chopped fresh mint leaves, or cilantro, for garnishing

❶ If using dried chick-peas, cook over medium heat in boiling unsalted water to cover generously until tender, about 1½ hours. Drain.

❷ Heat the oil in a flameproof casserole or large heavy saucepan over high heat. Add enough of the lamb to cover the base of the pan sparsely and cook, stirring frequently, until evenly browned. Remove the browned meat and continue cooking in batches, adding a little more oil if needed. When the last batch is nearly browned, add the onion and garlic, and cook, stirring frequently, for 2 minutes. Return all the meat to the pan and add the wine, if using, water, thyme, oregano, bay leaf, cinnamon and cumin. Bring just to a boil, skimming off any foam as it rises to the surface, reduce the heat to low and simmer for about 1½ hours until the meat is very tender. Discard the bay leaf.

❸ Stir in the chick-peas, tomatoes or tomato juice, roasted peppers, saffron or turmeric, leek, carrot and potato, and simmer for 15 minutes. Add the zucchini and peas, and continue simmering for 15–20 minutes more, or until all the vegetables are tender. Taste and adjust the seasoning, adding a little harissa, if you like a spicier soup.

❹ Ladle the soup into a warmed tureen or bowls and sprinkle with mint or cilantro.

GEORGIAN SPICY BEEF SOUP
with PLUMS

This slightly sour soup from the former Soviet Union, *kharcho*, appears in many versions. It is often flavored with dried plums, but fresh plums add the needed tartness and are easier to find. Fenugreek is an essential ingredient for authenticity, but its unusual taste is not pleasing to everyone and it can be difficult to obtain. Do not hesitate to try the soup with or without it.

SERVES 6

4 garlic cloves
5 allspice berries
10 peppercorns
15 coriander seeds
½ teaspoon fenugreek seeds
½ teaspoon crushed red pepper
　flakes
2 pounds boneless stewing beef,
　cut in 1-inch cubes
2 onions, finely chopped
1 carrot, finely chopped
large bouquet garni (2 bay
　leaves, coriander and
　parsley stems, thyme and
　savory sprigs and celery
　leaves)
10 cups water
2 teaspoons vegetable oil

2 garlic cloves, minced
6 tomatoes, preferably plum,
　peeled, seeded and chopped
6 large plums, stoned, peeled
　and finely chopped
½ teaspoon dried summer
　savory
½ teaspoon dried fenugreek
　leaves, crushed
¼ teaspoon turmeric
¼ teaspoon hot paprika, or a
　pinch of cayenne pepper
salt
lemon juice, to taste
1–2 tablespoons plum
　preserves (optional)
3 tablespoons chopped cilantro,
　to garnish

❶ Lightly crush 2 of the garlic cloves and put them in a piece of cheesecloth with the allspice berries, peppercorns, coriander and fenugreek seeds, and red pepper flakes. Tie with string.
❷ Put the cubes of beef in a flameproof casserole or large saucepan with half the onions and the carrot. Add the *bouquet garni*, spice bag and water. Bring to a boil over medium-high heat, skimming off any foam as it rises to the surface. Reduce the heat to low and simmer, partially covered, for 1½–2 hours until the meat is very tender, skimming as necessary and stirring occasionally.
❸ Strain the cooking liquid and discard the vegetables, *bouquet garni* and spice bag. Remove the meat from the bones and discard the fat, cartilage and bones. Spoon off the fat from the cooking liquid. (If preparing the recipe in advance, chill the meat until needed. Cool the cooking liquid and refrigerate, covered; remove the fat when it is congealed and hard.)
❹ Heat the oil in a large saucepan, add the remaining onions and cook over medium heat until just softened, about 3 minutes. Add the garlic, tomatoes, plums, savory, dried fenugreek, turmeric, paprika or cayenne and a little salt, and continue cooking for 5 minutes, stirring frequently. Add the beef and its cooking liquid, bring to a boil, reduce the heat to low and simmer for about 45 minutes, stirring occasionally.
❺ Taste and adjust the seasoning and stir in a few drops of lemon juice, or as needed, and if you wish, the plum preserves. (The soup should be slightly sour.) Ladle into warm bowls and sprinkle with cilantro.

POACHED BEEF *and* VEGETABLE SOUP

(Boeuf à la nage)

This elegant soup is a sophisticated and speedy version of *pot au feu*, the long-simmered classic of French country cooking. Select very small vegetables or cut larger ones into sticks or other small bite-size shapes. The stock should be rich and flavorful. Reduce weak stock to concentrate the flavor before using.

SERVES 4

4 cups beef stock	*1 baby cabbage, quartered*
2-3 tablespoons dry sherry or red wine	*6 dwarf squashes, halved*
	16 sugar snap peas
12 ounces beef fillet, about 2½ inches thick, tied	*1 tablespoon chopped fresh parsley*
16 small new carrots	*1 tablespoon chopped fresh chives*
12–16 small new potatoes	
16 small button mushrooms	

❶ In a medium saucepan, bring the stock to a boil, add the sherry or wine and reduce the heat to medium-low. Add the beef, carrots, potatoes and mushrooms, and simmer for 5 minutes. Add the cabbage and continue cooking for 7 minutes. Add the squashes and peas, and continue cooking for 4–5 minutes.

❷ Transfer the meat to a chopping board. Test the vegetables to make sure they are cooked, as cooking time varies slightly depending on their size. Continue simmering, if necessary, until they are cooked. Remove the vegetables and bring the stock to a boil.

❸ Cut the meat in half lengthwise and slice each half into pieces about ⅛-inch thick. (It should be very rare, as it will continue cooking in the stock.) Divide the meat among warm shallow soup plates or bowls and arrange the vegetables evenly. Ladle over the boiling stock and sprinkle with herbs.

~·~·~·~·~·~·~·~·~·~

TO DRINK
A medium-bodied
cru bourgeois red
Bordeaux.

~·~·~·~·~·~·~·~·~·~

PORK *and* HOMINY SOUP

(Posole)

Dried corn kernels treated with lime to soften the outer hull are known as hominy, or in the south west of the US, posole. The process, which improves the nutritional value of the grain, goes back to the Mayans and Aztecs, native civilizations of South America. Canned hominy may be used if the dried variety is not available. Sometimes tomatoes are omitted from the soup and tomato salsa is added at the table. The crispy vegetable garnishes provide a pleasing element of contrast.

SERVES 4

12 ounces boneless pork, cut in ¾-inch cubes	*1½ cups chopped canned tomatoes in juice*
juice of 1 lime	*1–2 roasted ancho chilies, seeds and core discarded, chopped, or ¼ teaspoon crushed red pepper flakes*
4 garlic cloves, minced	
1¾ cups dried corn (posole), soaked for 3–12 hours, or 3½ cups (1¼ pounds) canned hominy, rinsed and drained	
	salt
1 tablespoon rendered pork fat or vegetable oil	TO GARNISH
	sour cream
2½ cups chicken stock	*shredded iceberg lettuce*
¾ teaspoon dried oregano	*chopped scallions*
¾ teaspoon ground cumin	*sliced radishes*
	lime wedges

❶ Put the pork in a shallow glass or ceramic dish, add the lime juice and half the garlic, and stir to coat. Leave to marinate for 2–12 hours.

❷ If using dried corn, cook over medium heat in boiling unsalted water to cover generously until just tender, 1–2 hours. Drain.

❸ Strain and reserve the marinade. Scrape off and discard the garlic and pat the meat dry. Heat the fat or oil in a flame-proof casserole or large heavy saucepan over medium-high heat. Brown the meat, in batches if necessary, not crowding the pan and turning to color evenly. When all the meat is browned, return to the pan and add the stock, oregano, cumin and the remaining garlic. Reduce the heat to low and simmer for about 45 minutes, or until the meat is tender. Stir in the tomatoes, the drained cooked or canned hominy, chilies and salt to taste. Bring to a boil, reduce the heat to low and simmer for 20–30 minutes longer.

❹ Ladle into a warm tureen or bowls and serve with sour cream, lettuce, scallions, radishes and lime wedges.

RABBIT *and* LEEK SOUP *with* PRUNES

Agen is the centre of prune production in France and there you can find many dishes combining prunes with meat, poultry and even fish. Rabbit is traditionally paired with prunes. If you are able to obtain a wild rabbit, the flavor of the soup will be more robust.

SERVES 6

3 large leeks
1 tablespoon vegetable oil
2 pounds rabbit pieces
6 tablespoons dry white wine
2 cups water
3 garlic cloves, crushed

4–5 fresh thyme sprigs, or
½ teaspoon dried thyme
bay leaf
6 cups chicken stock
18 stoned prunes, about
6 ounces
salt and freshly ground pepper

❶ Thinly slice the white part of the leeks and reserve. Chop the green parts.

❷ Heat the oil in a large flameproof casserole over medium-high heat. Add the rabbit pieces and cook until golden brown, turning to color evenly. Add the wine and water, bring to a boil and add the chopped green part of the leeks, garlic and herbs. Add the stock, reduce the heat to low, cover and simmer very gently for about 1 hour until the rabbit is very tender. (Wild rabbit may take longer.) Strain the cooking liquid and discard the vegetables and herbs. When cool enough to handle, take the rabbit meat from the bones.

❸ Remove as much fat as possible from the cooking liquid and put it in a large saucepan with the rabbit meat, sliced leeks and prunes. Season with salt and pepper to taste. Bring to a boil over medium-high heat, reduce the heat to low and simmer gently, stirring occasionally, until the leeks are tender. Taste and adjust the seasoning, if needed, and ladle the soup into a warm tureen or bowls.

~.~.~.~.~.~.~.~.~

TO DRINK
A medium-dry fruity
rosé, especially one
from the south west
of France.

~.~.~.~.~.~.~.~.~

VINTNERS' OXTAIL SOUP

Grapes were among the earliest cultivated plants and, while used primarily for wine, they have also featured in the kitchen, especially in medieval cooking. The contemporary revival of the fashion for combining fruit with meat, poultry or fish owes its popularity to the *nouvelle cuisine* movement of the 1970s. If you start this soup the day before, it is easy to remove all the fat from the rich stock.

SERVES 4–6

*3 pounds oxtails, cut in
   2-inch pieces*
2 small onions, quartered
2 carrots, cut in chunks
4–5 garlic cloves
salt and freshly ground pepper
4 tablespoons dry white wine
6 cups water
*large bouquet garni (parsley
   stems, thyme and bay leaf)*

1 tablespoon butter
*4 ounces button mushrooms,
   thinly sliced*
1 small leek, thinly sliced
*grated zest of ½ lemon
   (unwaxed or scrubbed)*
*5 ounces seedless white grapes
   (about 30), skinned, if
   wished, and halved*
lemon juice, to taste (optional)

❶ Preheat the oven to 425°F. Remove as much fat as possible from the oxtails. Put them in a shallow roasting pan with the onions, carrots and garlic. Season lightly with salt and pepper, and roast, turning and stirring occasionally, for 30–40 minutes until well browned.

❷ Transfer the meat and vegetables to a large flameproof casserole or stockpot. Spoon off as much fat as possible from the roasting pan, set over high heat and add the white wine. Bring to the boil, stirring and scraping the bottom of the tin. Pour the liquid into the casserole or stockpot. Add the water and bouquet garni. Bring just to a boil, reduce the heat to low and simmer very gently, partially covered, for 3–4 hours until the meat is very tender. Using a slotted spoon, remove the oxtails. Strain the cooking liquid and discard the vegetables.

❸ Cool the cooking liquid and chill, covered. Remove the meat from the oxtails and discard the fat, cartilage and bone. Chill the meat until needed.

❹ Remove and discard the congealed fat from the cooking liquid. Melt the butter in a large saucepan over medium heat. Add the mushrooms and cook until lightly browned, about 5 minutes. Stir in the leeks and cook until just softened, about 5 minutes longer. Add the cooking liquid, lemon zest, grapes, and the reserved meat. Bring just to a boil, reduce the heat to medium-low and simmer for 10–15 minutes, or until the soup is hot and the grapes are tender. Taste and adjust the seasoning, adding a few drops of lemon juice, if wished. Ladle into warm bowls.

~.~.~.~.~.~.~.~.~.~
To Drink
A fruity powerful
white wine, such as
Gewürztraminer.

~.~.~.~.~.~.~.~.~.~

ITALIAN SAUSAGE *and* ZUCCHINI SOUP

This soup emphasizes the fennel used to flavor many Italian sausages. If other sausages are used, add a pinch of fennel seeds to the soup. The lemon, garlic and parsley seasoning, or *gremolata*, a traditional garnish for stews and seafood, brings a pleasant zing to the soup.

SERVES 4–6

1 pound sweet Italian sausages
1 tablespoon olive oil
1 large onion, finely chopped
2 garlic cloves, minced
1 fennel bulb, finely chopped
½ red or yellow bell pepper, seeded and finely chopped
1 pound zucchini, coarsely grated
6 cups brown chicken or beef stock
1 teaspoon chopped fresh marjoram, or ¼ teaspoon dried
1 teaspoon chopped fresh thyme, or ¼ teaspoon dried
bay leaf
salt and freshly ground pepper
LEMON-GARLIC SEASONING
grated zest of ½ lemon (unwaxed or scrubbed)
1 garlic clove, minced
2 tablespoons chopped parsley

❶ Put the sausages in a frying pan and set over medium heat. Cook until well browned, turning to colour evenly. Remove and drain on paper towels. Cut into slices.
❷ Heat the oil in a heavy saucepan or flameproof casserole over medium-high heat. Add the onion, garlic, fennel and pepper, and cook for 3–4 minutes, stirring occasionally, until slightly softened.
❸ Add the zucchini, stock and herbs. Stir in the sliced sausages, reduce the heat to low and simmer for about 20 minutes. Add a little stock or water if you like a thinner soup. Season to taste with salt, if needed, and pepper. Discard the bay leaf.
❹ For the lemon-garlic seasoning, chop together the lemon zest, garlic and parsley until very fine and stir into the soup. Heat through and ladle into a warm tureen or bowl.

~.~.~.~.~.~.~.~.~.~

TO DRINK
Most medium-bodied fruity Italian red wines, such as a good Valpolicella.

~.~.~.~.~.~.~.~.~.~

~.~.~.~.~.~.~.~.~.~

COOK'S TIP
This is a good way to use a large zucchini. If the skin is very tough, peel before grating.

~.~.~.~.~.~.~.~.~.~

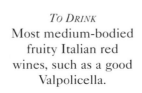

MEATBALL SOUP *with* CABBAGE *and* PARMESAN CHEESE

These flavorful meatballs can be shaped and browned ahead, so the final preparation of the soup is easier. Make them quite small so they are really bite-sized.

SERVES 8

1 large onion, halved
4–5 tablespoons olive oil
1 garlic clove, finely minced
1 cup soft bread crumbs
1 pound lean ground
*   beef or veal*
1 egg, lightly beaten
¼ teaspoon chopped fresh thyme
*   leaves, or ¼ teaspoon dried*
¼ teaspoon chopped fresh
*   marjoram leaves, or*
*   ¼ teaspoon dried*

2 tablespoons freshly grated
*   Parmesan cheese, plus more*
*   for serving*
salt and freshly ground pepper
flour, for coating
12 ounces young green cabbage,
*   cored, quartered and thinly*
*   sliced*
1½ pounds tomatoes, peeled,
*   seeded and chopped*
4 cups brown chicken
*   or beef stock*

❶ Chop half the onion finely. Slice the other half thinly and reserve. Heat 2 teaspoons of the oil in a small frying pan over medium heat and cook the chopped onion until just softened, about 3 minutes, stirring frequently. Add the garlic and continue cooking for 2 minutes longer. Remove from the heat and allow to cool slightly.

❷ Put the breadcrumbs in a small bowl and cover with water. Let stand for 2 minutes, drain and squeeze dry. In a mixing bowl, combine the bread crumbs, chopped onion, meat, egg, thyme, marjoram and Parmesan cheese. Season with salt, if needed, and plenty of pepper. Mix thoroughly and roll into small balls about ¾ inch in diameter. Roll the balls in flour to coat lightly.

❸ Heat 2 tablespoons of the remaining oil in a large frying pan over medium-high heat. Brown the meatballs in batches, not crowding the pan and turning to color evenly. Remove and drain on paper towels. (Refrigerate, if making in advance.)

❹ Heat the remaining oil in a large saucepan over medium heat. Add the reserved onion slices and cabbage, and cook for 3–4 minutes, stirring frequently, until they start to wilt. Add the tomatoes, stock and meatballs. Bring to a boil, reduce the heat to medium-low and simmer for about 20 minutes, or until the vegetables are tender. Taste and adjust the seasoning if necessary. Ladle into warm bowls and serve sprinkled with Parmesan cheese.

~.~.~.~.~.~.~.~.~.~

TO DRINK
A good
Crianza Rioja or
Chianti.

~.~.~.~.~.~.~.~.~.~

TEXAS CHILI

This popular style of fiery soup probably came about of necessity in a cattle drive chuckwagon. Now it offers scope for almost limitless variation. This recipe is equally good made with pork or venison instead of beef. If you like, serve cooked and seasoned kidney or pinto beans to accompany.

SERVES 8

2 red bell peppers
2 fresh ancho or Jalapeño chilies
3½ pounds lean beef (chuck steak)
3 tablespoons olive oil
2 large sweet onions, finely chopped
4–5 garlic cloves
½ cup red wine
1 cup tomato paste
3 cups tomato juice
3 cups beef stock, or brown chicken stock

1 cup water, or more
large bouquet garni (bay leaf, coriander stems and thyme)
1 teaspoon cumin seeds, crushed
1 teaspoon dried oregano
salt
2 teaspoons chili powder, or to taste
sour cream, to garnish
chopped cilantro, for garnishing

❶ Preheat the oven to 400°F. Put the peppers and chilies in a baking dish at the top of the oven and roast for about 30–40 minutes, turning a quarter turn every 10 minutes, until the peppers are wrinkly and the skin has begun to darken. Put them in a plastic storage box or bag, close tightly and allow to steam for 30 minutes. Halve the peppers and remove the cores, seeds and skin. (Wear rubber gloves when handling chilies and avoid touching eyes or other sensitive areas.) Roughly chop the pepper flesh.

❷ Chop the beef very finely with a large knife or in a food processor fitted with a steel blade, working in small batches and pulsing to avoid puréeing the meat.

❸ Heat half the oil in a large frying pan over high heat. Add enough meat to cover the bottom of the pan sparsely and cook, stirring frequently, until evenly browned. Remove the browned meat to a large nonreactive saucepan and continue cooking in batches. When all the meat is browned, reduce the heat to medium and add the onions and garlic. Cook, stirring frequently, until they start to soften, 4–5 minutes. Add the wine and boil for 1 minute, stirring and scraping the bottom of the pan to dissolve the brown bits, and pour over the meat.

❹ Stir in the peppers and chilies, tomato paste, tomato juice, stock and water, adding more if needed to cover by at least 1 inch. Add the *bouquet garni*, cumin, oregano and salt to taste. Bring to a boil, reduce the heat to low and simmer, partially covered, for 1 hour. Stir in the chili powder and continue cooking for 30 minutes longer, or until the meat is very tender, stirring occasionally. Taste and adjust the seasoning, adding more chili powder, if wished.

❺ Ladle into warm bowls and serve garnished with sour cream and cilantro.

HAM *and* SPLIT PEA SOUP

This rich, thick soup is ideal for making in advance and the ham stock gives it an intensity of flavor. If time is short, omit making ham stock, use 4 cups each water and chicken stock, and add the *bouquet garni* to the soup, removing it before puréeing.

SERVES 6

2 cups (1 pound) split yellow peas
1 tablespoon butter
3 shallots or 1 small onion, finely chopped
1 large carrot, grated
1 small celery stalk with leaves, finely chopped
8 ounces smoked ham steak, trimmed of all fat and cut into small pieces
freshly ground pepper
1 teaspoon chopped fresh sage, or ¼ teaspoon dried thyme
3–4 tablespoons dry sherry (optional)
chopped fresh parsley, for garnishing

HAM STOCK

1½ pounds ham bones (ham hock, knuckle or shank), rinsed, and a chicken carcass (or 3–4 wings)
1 large onion, quartered and studded with 2 cloves
2 large carrots, sliced
2 celery stalks, sliced
4 garlic cloves
5 allspice berries
10 peppercorns
bouquet garni (2 bay leaves, 4–5 sage leaves, 1 small rosemary sprig, 3–4 thyme sprigs and parsley stems)
½ cup dry white wine
6 cups water

❶ To make the stock, put the ham bones and chicken carcass in a large pot with the studded onion, carrots, celery, garlic, allspice berries, peppercorns, *bouquet garni*, wine and water. Bring to a boil over medium-high heat, skimming off the foam as it rises to the surface. Reduce the heat to medium-low and simmer, partially covered, for about 3½ hours until flavorful and slightly reduced.

❷ Strain the stock and discard the vegetables, spices and herbs. Remove any meat from the ham bone and cut into small pieces. Discard all fat, cartilage and bone. Spoon off the fat from the stock. (If preparing in advance, refrigerate the meat until needed. Cool the stock and refrigerate, covered; remove the fat when it is congealed.)

❸ Rinse the split peas under cold running water. Melt the butter in a large flameproof casserole or stockpot over medium heat. Add the shallots or onion and cook until just softened, about 3 minutes, stirring occasionally. Add the carrot and celery, and continue cooking for 2 minutes. Add the peas, ham stock and any meat from the stock bones.

Season with plenty of pepper and simmer gently for about 1 hour, or until the peas are soft.

❹ Purée the soup, in batches if necessary, in a blender or a food processor fitted with a steel blade, or pass it through a food mill fitted with a fine disk.

❺ Return the soup to a large saucepan and stir in the ham and sage or thyme. Thin with water if you like a thinner soup, and simmer gently over low heat for about 30 minutes. Stir in the sherry, if using, and heat through. Taste and adjust the seasoning. Ladle into a warm tureen or individual soup bowls and garnish with parsley.

~·~·~·~·~·~·~·~·~·~

To Drink
Well chilled Fino
sherry or an oaky
white wine.

~·~·~·~·~·~·~·~·~·~

CHAPTER THREE

Poultry
and Game
Soups

An elixir of health, a comforter of miseries, chicken soup seems to have mystical properties, and we consume it with reverence as well as relish. When it comes to goodness, game birds are equally well suited for soup-making, when slow simmering highlights the exotic flavors and tenderizes at the same time.

POULTRY *and* GAME SOUPS

*C*hicken soup is soothing, satisfying and invigorating. It is good either plain or fancy and its curative properties are well documented. In fact, it is sometimes known as "Jewish penicillin." The most international soup of all, it also features in Chinese, French, Spanish, Italian, Mexican, American and almost all other cuisines.

Chicken stock is used in soup-making more often than any other because it amalgamates and supports the flavors of the other ingredients, whether they are delicate, like ground almonds, or robust, like broccoli rabe. It is quicker to cook than meat stock and you will have the makings of two meals if you use a whole bird instead of just trimmings and bones to make the stock, providing cooked chicken for a salad or casserole – or to serve in chicken soup!

Other poultry stocks are equally delicious and may be substituted for chicken stock, unless they are particularly gamey. Then they are better enjoyed on their own or with a little of the meat in them, as in Pheasant Soup.

The versatility of poultry-based

56

The most flavorful chicken soups are those made from mature barnyard birds – an old hen is really best. Larger birds may be tough, but in long-simmered soup, that is not a problem. Wing tips and giblets add extra flavor to poultry stocks.

soups is limitless. They run the gamut from heartwarming traditional favourites like Chicken Soup with Herb Dumplings to novel creations such as Turkey Chili, from foreign classics like Chinese Chicken and Corn Soup to mainstream staples like Chicken Soup with Homemade Noodles. They thrive with sultry spices or subtle seasoning, and you can change the nature of the soup by varying the ingredients you add and the garnishes you use. These are soups for all occasions to be enjoyed by everyone.

The potential of poultry in soup-making is boundless. Explore the possibilities offered by chicken, turkey, duck, pheasant and other game birds.

~.~.~.~.~.~.~.~.~.~

"Fesaunt exceedeth all foules in sweetnesse and wholesomenesse, and is equal to a capon in nourishment . . . It is meate for Princes and great estates, and for poor Schollers when they can get it."

THE CASTEL OF HELTH
1539, Sir Thomas Elyot

~·~·~·~·~·~·~·~·~

CHICKEN VELVET SOUP *with* ALMOND BALLS

The silky texture and elegant nature of this soup make it perfect for entertaining. A flavorful stock with all fat removed is essential. If you wish, make the almond balls a few hours beforehand and reheat them in a moderate oven for serving.

SERVES 6

1¼ cups blanched whole almonds	3 eggs, separated
⅔ cup milk	vegetable oil, for frying
¾ cup fresh white bread crumbs	6 cups chicken stock
	3 tablespoons cornstarch
salt and white pepper	¼ cup whipping cream
	freshly grated nutmeg

❶ In a food processor fitted with a steel blade, process the almonds until finely ground. Put in a small saucepan and pour over the milk. Set over medium-high heat until bubbles appear around the edge. Remove from the heat and allow to stand for 30 minutes. Strain and reserve the almonds and milk separately.

❷ To make the almond balls, combine the bread crumbs and reserved ground almonds with a pinch of salt in a small bowl. Beat the egg whites in a shallow bowl until frothy. Stir enough of the egg whites into the almond-breadcrumb mixture to make it stick together. Form into small balls about ½ inch in diameter. Roll the balls in the remaining egg white and place on a wire rack until all are coated. In a frying pan, add oil to a depth of about ¼ inch. Heat over medium-high heat until hot. Fry the balls, a few at a time, turning to color evenly. Drain on paper towels. Keep warm in a moderately slow oven.

❸ Combine the chicken stock and reserved almond milk in a large heavy-based saucepan and place over medium heat until the liquid begins to tremble. In a medium bowl, whisk together the egg yolks, add the cornstarch and cream and whisk until smooth. Whisk in a quarter of the hot stock mixture, then pour it all back into the saucepan, whisking constantly. With a wooden spoon, stir over medium-low heat until the soup begins to thicken, about 15 minutes (do not allow to boil or mixture may curdle). Season to taste with salt, pepper and nutmeg. Ladle into warm shallow soup plates and garnish with almond balls.

TURKEY *and* WILD RICE SOUP

Most turkey soups have been devised as a way of using leftover turkey, and this recipe can serve that purpose with a new twist. Try to remember to roast the garlic with the turkey, or put it in the oven to bake with something else. It needs about 30 minutes in a 400°F oven and will keep refrigerated for 2–3 days. The fried sage leaves echo the holiday theme, but if you prefer, garnish with chopped fresh tarragon or parsley instead.

SERVES 4

1 head garlic, wrapped in foil and roasted until soft	salt and freshly ground pepper
6 cups turkey stock	1 cup cooked wild rice
4 ounces oyster mushrooms, or other flavorful wild or cultivated mushrooms	1 cup chopped cooked turkey
	oil, for frying
	12–16 fresh sage leaves, for garnishing
1 tablespoon butter	

❶ Put the garlic and stock in a large saucepan over medium heat and bring to a boil slowly over medium heat. Reduce the heat to low and simmer gently, partially covered, for about 20 minutes, or until the garlic has flavored the stock.

❷ Meanwhile, cut the mushrooms into thin strips or slices. Melt the butter in a frying pan over medium heat. Add the mushrooms, season lightly with salt and pepper, and cook, stirring gently and frequently, until lightly browned.

❸ Remove the garlic from the stock with a slotted spoon. (If you wish, it can be used to flavor something else.) Stir in the rice, turkey and mushrooms and simmer for 10–15 minutes.

❹ Pour enough oil into a small frying pan to cover the bottom generously. Set over high heat until the oil starts to smoke. Add the sage leaves and fry until crispy, about 20 seconds. Drain on paper towels.

❺ Ladle the soup into a warm tureen or soup bowls and garnish with the sage leaves.

TURKEY CHILI

Chili comes in all colors and this green, relatively mild chili has a creamy richness and appealing complexity.

SERVES 6

1 tablespoon butter
1 pound skinless boneless turkey, finely chopped or minced
1 onion, finely chopped
2 celery stalks, finely chopped
1 green bell pepper, cored, seeded and finely chopped
2 garlic cloves, minced
1 green chili pepper, cored, seeded and finely chopped
4 cups turkey or chicken stock
½ teaspoon chili powder, or to taste (optional)
4 tablespoons extra-virgin olive oil
½ cup blanched almonds
½ cup stoned green olives
salt and freshly ground pepper
1 bunch parsley, stems removed

❶ Melt the butter in a flameproof casserole or large saucepan over medium heat. Add the turkey and cook, stirring frequently, until lightly browned, about 5 minutes. Stir in the onion, celery and green pepper, and cook until softened. Add the garlic and chili pepper, and continue cooking for 2–3 minutes, stirring constantly.

❷ Stir in the stock and bring just to a boil. Reduce the heat to medium-low and simmer for 5 minutes. Taste and add chili powder if you like it hotter.

❸ Meanwhile, put the oil, almonds, olives and half the parsley in a food processor fitted with a steel blade and process until puréed. Stir the green purée into the soup, season with salt and pepper to taste and simmer, covered, for 20 minutes.

❹ Finely chop the remaining parsley. Ladle the chili into a warm tureen or bowls and sprinkle with chopped parsley.

CHINESE CHICKEN *and* CORN SOUP

This Chinese soup is appreciated around the world. The delicate flavors and subtle spicing make it an approachable and suitably light starter for entertaining, not to be reserved just for Oriental meals.

SERVES 6

6 cups chicken stock
2 boneless skinless chicken
    breasts
1 small onion, roughly chopped
1 carrot, roughly chopped
1 celery stalk, roughly chopped
1-inch piece fresh gingerroot,
    peeled and sliced
bouquet garni (parsley stems,
    leek greens and bay leaf)
4 ears corn, or 2½ cups thawed

frozen or canned
    corn kernels
3 tablespoons cornstarch, or
    4 tablespoons if using
    kernels (see Cook's Tip below)
8 spring onions
salt and white pepper
2 egg whites, beaten with
    3 tablespoons water
2 ounces cooked ham, cut into
    matchstick strips

❶ Put the stock in a large saucepan with the chicken, onion, carrot, celery, ginger and *bouquet garni*. Bring to a boil over medium-high heat, skimming off any foam as it rises to the surface. Reduce the heat to medium-low and simmer, partially covered, for 30–40 minutes, or until the chicken is very tender. Strain the stock, remove the chicken and discard the vegetables. Shred the chicken.

❷ Cut the kernels from the corn, without cutting down to the cob. With the back of a knife, scrape the cobs to extract the milky liquid from the base of kernels.

❸ Combine the strained stock, half the spring onions and the corn kernels and their liquid, if available, in the saucepan, and season with salt and white pepper. Bring to a boil slowly over medium heat and boil gently for 5 minutes.

❹ Stir the cornstarch into 3 tablespoons cold water until dissolved and pour into the soup, stirring constantly. Cook, stirring, until the soup thickens, about 5 minutes. Slowly pour the egg whites into the soup while stirring vigorously. Add the ham and shredded chicken, and heat through, 1–2 minutes. Ladle into warm bowls and garnish with the remaining spring onions.

~.~.~.~.~.~.~.~.~.~

COOK'S TIP
If you are using frozen or canned corn, it will not thicken the soup as much as the starchy liquid from the corn, so increase the amount of cornstarch to 4 tablespoons.

~.~.~.~.~.~.~.~.~.~

CHICKEN SOUP *with* HERB DUMPLINGS

The secret of light dumplings is simmering them very gently on top of the liquid and not peeking. The herbs to flavor them can vary according to what you have available, but fresh herbs give the best color and flavor.

SERVES 6

4-pound chicken, quartered
10 cups water
2 celery stalks, sliced
2 carrots, sliced
3 shallots or 1 onion, sliced
2 leeks, slit lengthwise and
   sliced
2–3 garlic cloves, crushed
1 onion, studded with 3 cloves
2 teaspoons peppercorns
2 allspice berries
large bouquet garni (parsley
   stems, thyme and tarragon
   sprigs, and bay leaf)
salt and freshly ground pepper
pinch saffron threads, soaked

in 2 tablespoons hot water
   (optional)
3 tablespoons butter
4 tablespoons flour
DUMPLINGS
1 cup flour
1 teaspoon baking powder
¼ teaspoon salt
1 tablespoon soft butter
1 tablespoon chopped fresh
   parsley
1 tablespoon chopped fresh
   tarragon, or mixed chives
   and thyme
1 egg yolk
3 tablespoons milk

COOK'S TIP
To prepare in advance,
cook the chicken and refrigerate
the chicken and stock separately.
Remove any congealed fat from
the stock and reheat gently before
continuing. If making the
soup all at once, the dumplings
can be prepared an hour or so
beforehand, while the chicken
is cooking, and kept in the
refrigerator, covered,
until needed.

❶ Put the chicken in a large saucepan with the water, celery, carrots, shallots or onion, leeks, garlic and studded onion. Wrap the peppercorns and allspice berries in a piece of cheesecloth and tie with string. Add the spice bag and *bouquet garni* with a little salt. If needed, add more water to cover the ingredients. Bring just to a boil over medium-high heat, skimming off the foam as it rises to the surface. Reduce the heat to medium-low and simmer, partially covered, for about 1½ hours until the chicken is tender, skimming from time to time.

❷ Remove the chicken with a slotted spoon and set aside to cool. Add the saffron, if using, to the stock and continue simmering, uncovered. Skin the chicken and take the meat from the bones; discard the skin and bones. Cut the meat into large pieces and reserve.

❸ Remove as much fat as possible from the stock and strain into a large measuring container: there should be about 8 cups. Reduce the stock if necessary. Discard the studded onion, *bouquet garni* and spice bag, and reserve the cooking vegetables.

❹ In a large heavy saucepan, melt the butter over medium-high heat. Stir in the flour and cook for 2–3 minutes until it starts to color. Gradually pour in a quarter of the stock, whisking constantly. Bring to a boil, whisking, and cook for 2 minutes. Whisk in the remaining stock and when it comes back to a boil, reduce the heat to medium-low, add the reserved chicken and vegetables, and season to taste. Simmer, stirring occasionally, for 5–10 minutes.

❺ For the dumplings, sift the flour, baking powder and salt into a bowl. Cut or rub in the butter until the mixture looks like coarse crumbs. Add the herbs. Beat together the egg yolk and milk, and stir into the flour mixture to form a soft dough, adding a little more milk, if needed.

❻ Drop the dumpling dough by rounded teaspoonfuls into the simmering soup. Cover the pan tightly and cook for 8–10 minutes, or until the dumplings are swollen and fluffy. Ladle into warm soup plates.

CHICKEN MINESTRONE

This chunky Mediterranean-style soup is full of goodness. You can substitute other vegetables if you wish, such as flat Italian green beans, cut in pieces, or diced celeriac.

SERVES 8–10

¾ cup (5 ounces) dried
    cannellini or borlotti beans,
    soaked overnight
4 garlic cloves, minced
bouquet garni (parsley stems,
    thyme sprigs, rosemary
    sprig and bay leaf)
1 tablespoon olive oil
1 onion, finely chopped
10 cups chicken stock
2 cups cubed cooked chicken
3 cups diced pumpkin

1 leek, thinly sliced
2 sage leaves, finely chopped, or
    ¼ teaspoon dried
salt and freshly ground pepper
4 cups (6 ounces) broccoli rabe,
    leaves cut into ribbons,
    stems peeled and cut in
    ¾-inch pieces
3 small zucchini, halved
    lengthwise and sliced
1 cup small pasta shapes

❶ Drain the beans, put in a saucepan with cold water to cover and set over high heat. Bring to a boil and boil for 10 minutes. Drain, rinse and return to the pan. Add half the garlic and the *bouquet garni*, and cover generously with fresh water. Bring to a boil, reduce the heat to low and simmer until tender, 1–1½ hours, adding boiling water as needed to keep the beans covered by at least 1 inch. Discard the *bouquet garni*.

❷ Heat the oil in a large heavy saucepan over medium heat and add the onion. Cook for 2–3 minutes until slightly softened, stirring occasionally, then add the remaining garlic and continue cooking for 2 minutes, stirring frequently. Add the stock, the beans and their cooking liquid, chicken, pumpkin, leek and sage, and season to taste with salt and pepper. Bring to a boil, reduce the heat to medium-low and simmer for 5 minutes. Stir in the broccoli rabe, courgettes and pasta, and continue cooking for 15–20 minutes longer, or until the pasta and all the vegetables are tender.

❸ Taste and adjust the seasoning, and ladle the soup into warm bowls.

SMOKED CHICKEN *and* LENTIL SOUP

Lentils are often paired with ham, as smoked meats seem to give a pleasing element of richness. Smoked chicken, or other smoked poultry or game, offers a more subtle and complex combination of flavors.

SERVES 4

1 tablespoon butter
2 leeks, split and thinly sliced
2 carrots, finely chopped
1 large onion, finely chopped
1 garlic clove, minced
1 cup dried lentils (preferably
    Puy)
2 cups water

bouquet garni (thyme sprigs,
    celery leaves, sage and
    bay leaf)
4 cups chicken stock
1⅓ cups cubed smoked chicken
salt and freshly ground
    pepper

❶ Melt the butter in a large saucepan or stockpot over medium heat. Add the leeks, carrots, onion and garlic, and cook for 4–5 minutes until slightly softened, stirring frequently.

❷ Rinse and drain the lentils, and check for any small stones. Add to the vegetables with the water and *bouquet garni*. Bring to a boil, reduce the heat to medium-low and simmer for about 30 minutes, or until the lentils are just tender.

❸ Add the chicken, season to taste with salt and pepper, and continue cooking for 15 minutes. Remove the *bouquet garni* and ladle into a warm tureen or bowls.

~.~.~.~.~.~.~.~.~.~

TO DRINK
An oaky Chardonnay
or a light dry red
wine.

~·~·~·~·~·~·~·~·~

CHICKEN SOUP *with* HOMEMADE NOODLES

These rich golden egg noodles are worth the effort, but if time is short, save noodle-making for another day and simmer good quality bought fresh pasta in the soup. Scientific studies indicate that chicken soup, long held to be a panacea for minor ailments, does have certain restorative properties – but don't reserve this soup for illness!

SERVES 6

4 chicken leg quarters, about 1¾ pounds, skinned	5 ounces mushrooms, sliced
8 cups chicken stock	2 tablespoons chopped fresh parsley
1 celery stalk, roughly chopped	NOODLES
1 carrot, roughly chopped	1 cup flour
1 onion, sliced	¼ teaspoon salt
1 garlic clove, crushed	2 egg yolks
5 peppercorns	1 teaspoon extra-virgin olive oil
large bouquet garni (parsley stems, thyme sprigs and bay leaf)	pinch saffron threads, soaked in 2 tablespoons hot water
1 tablespoon butter	

❶ For the noodles, put the flour and salt into a food processor fitted with a steel blade and pulse to combine. In a small bowl, beat together the egg yolks and oil, strain in the saffron liquid and beat to mix; discard the threads. With the machine running, pour in the egg yolk mixture and continue running until it all comes together and forms a ball which leaves the bowl virtually clean. If this doesn't happen and the dough seems a bit sticky, add 2 tablespoons of flour and continue kneading in the food processor until it forms a ball and the dough does not stick to your hands. Wrap and chill for at least 30 minutes.

❷ Divide the dough into quarters and roll out on a lightly floured surface as thinly as possible, less than ¹⁄₁₆ inch, and cut into diamond shapes about 1½ inches on each side. Alternatively, use a pasta machine to roll the dough into wide strips and cut them into noodles about ⅜ inch wide. Let the noodles dry in a single layer on floured wire racks or baking trays for about 1 hour. (If making ahead, leave to dry for about 3 hours and store in a plastic bag, refrigerated, for up to 1 day.)

❸ Put the chicken in a large saucepan with the stock, celery, carrot, onion, garlic, peppercorns and *bouquet garni*. Bring just to a boil over medium-high heat, skimming off the foam as it rises to the surface. Reduce the heat to medium-low and simmer, partially covered, for about 45 minutes, or until the chicken is tender, skimming as needed.

❹ Remove the chicken from the stock and set aside to cool. Continue simmering the stock, uncovered, for about 30 minutes. When the chicken is cool enough to handle, take the meat from the bones and cut into bite-sized pieces. Strain the stock and remove as much fat as possible; discard the *bouquet garni* and vegetables.

❺ Melt the butter in a large saucepan or flameproof casserole over medium heat. Add the mushrooms and 1 tablespoon of water and cook until lightly browned, stirring frequently. Add the stock and bring to a boil. Stir in the noodles and boil gently for 10 minutes. Return the chicken to the stock and continue cooking for 5–10 minutes longer, or until the noodles are tender. Ladle the soup into warm shallow bowls and sprinkle with parsley.

PHEASANT SOUP *with* LIVER DUMPLINGS

This soup is great for gourmet hunters! Make it after roasting pheasant, using leftover cooked meat and stock made from the carcasses, or make stock from the remaining parts of raw birds after the breasts have been removed for serving separately.

SERVES 4

6 cups pheasant stock
2 cups cubed cooked pheasant
1 tablespoon chopped fresh parsley
1 tablespoon chopped fresh chives and/or tarragon
LIVER DUMPLINGS
1 tablespoon butter, plus more for frying

1 shallot, finely chopped
⅓ cup (3½ ounces) pheasant or chicken livers
1 egg, beaten
1 tablespoon whipping cream
1 cup fresh white bread crumbs
1 teaspoon chopped fresh thyme
salt and freshly ground pepper

❶ Combine the stock and pheasant meat in a saucepan. Bring to a boil, reduce the heat to low and simmer for about 15 minutes.

❷ For the liver dumplings, melt half the butter in a small frying pan over medium-low heat and cook the shallots and garlic for 3–4 minutes until softened. Remove to cool. Add the remaining butter, increase the heat to medium-high and cook the livers for 2–3 minutes until browned, turning to color evenly. Remove and leave to cool slightly. Beat together the egg and cream in a small bowl. Add the bread crumbs, stir to combine and allow to stand until the bread has absorbed the egg, 1–2 minutes. Put the livers in a food processor fitted with a steel blade and pulse to chop finely. Add the thyme, shallots, garlic and soaked bread, and process to mix well.

❸ To cook the dumplings, melt a little butter in a frying pan over medium heat. Shape the mixture into small balls about the size of chestnuts. Flatten them slightly and fry gently until lightly browned, about 3 minutes, turning once. Drain on paper towels.

❹ Divide the dumplings among warm soup bowls. Ladle over the hot soup and sprinkle with herbs.

~.~.~.~.~.~.~.~.~

TO DRINK
Madeira or a fine old dry Oloroso sherry.

~·~·~·~·~·~·~·~·~

CURRIED CHICKEN CHOWDER

The subtle curry and slightly tart apple flavors give this soup a pleasing complexity that makes it suitable for the most elegant occasions, but equally appealing for a cosy lunch. The strength of curry powders varies, so use your own judgment, but it should not dominate.

SERVES 4

2 tablespoons butter
1 onion, finely chopped
1 garlic clove, minced
3 tablespoons flour
1 teaspoon curry powder
2 small carrots, halved lengthwise and thinly sliced
1 celery stalk, finely sliced
1 potato, diced
4 cups chicken stock

bouquet garni (parsley stems, thyme sprigs and bay leaf)
salt and freshly ground pepper
1 eating apple, peeled, cored and diced
2 cups cubed cooked chicken
4–6 tablespoons whipping cream
2 tablespoons chopped fresh chives, for garnishing

❶ Melt the butter in a large, heavy saucepan over medium heat. Add the onion and garlic. Cook, stirring frequently, until the vegetables start to soften, about 5 minutes. Stir in the flour and curry powder and cook for 2 minutes. Stir in the carrots, celery, potato and stock. Bring to a boil, stirring frequently. Add the *bouquet garni* and season with salt and pepper.

❷ Reduce the heat to medium-low and simmer, stirring occasionally, until the vegetables are almost tender, about 20 minutes. Add the apple and chicken, and continue cooking for about 10 minutes, or until the apple is tender. Remove the *bouquet garni*.

❸ Stir in the cream, taste and adjust the seasoning, and heat through. Ladle into warm bowls and garnish with chives.

~.~.~.~.~.~.~.~.~

TO DRINK
A well-chilled dry
Fino sherry.

~·~·~·~·~·~·~·~·~

CABBAGE AND BEAN SOUP
with PRESERVED DUCK *or* GOOSE

Cited by Curnonsky, the renowned French gastronome, as one of the four great regional dishes, this soup from Béarn, north of the Pyrenées, has many local and seasonal variations, such as the addition of Swiss chard or kale, chestnuts or garlic sausage. It should be thick enough for a spoon to stand upright and is usually cooked in a special earthenware kettle.

SERVES 8-10

2¼ *cups (1 pound) dried white beans, soaked overnight in cold water to cover generously*

3–4 *leg pieces preserved duck or goose (confit), with fat*

2 *onions, finely chopped*

1 *pound lean salt pork, rind removed, diced*

10 *cups duck or chicken stock, or water*

8 *ounces boneless pork shoulder*

bouquet garni (parsley stems, thyme and marjoram sprigs, and bay leaf)

1 *onion, studded with 3–4 cloves*

2 *leeks, halved lengthwise and finely sliced*

2 *carrots, sliced*

2 *white turnips, quartered*

4 *garlic cloves, minced*

salt and freshly ground pepper

1 *medium green cabbage, quartered*

3 *potatoes, cubed*

2 *tablespoons chopped fresh parsley*

TO SERVE

8–10 *large croutons (see page 122)*

⅔ *cup grated Gruyère cheese*

❶ Drain the beans, put in a saucepan with cold water to cover and set over high heat. Bring to a boil and boil for 10 minutes. Drain and add fresh cold water to cover. Bring to a boil again, drain and rinse well.

❷ Scrape the fat from the *confit* and reserve separately from the meat.

❸ Heat 3 tablespoons of the fat from the *confit* in a large flameproof casserole over medium-high heat. Add the chopped onions and salt pork and cook until lightly browned, stirring frequently. Add the beans, stock, pork, *bouquet garni* and studded onion. Simmer over low heat for 1 hour, skimming off the fat and stirring occasionally.

❹ Add the leeks, carrots, turnips and half the garlic and continue cooking for 20 minutes, or until the beans and meat are tender, stirring constantly. Taste and season with salt, if needed, and pepper.

❺ Bring a large saucepan of salted water to a boil and add the cabbage. Cook, uncovered, for 10 minutes, rinse under cold water and drain.

❻ Add the cabbage and potatoes to the beans with the cooked ham, the remaining garlic and the parsley. Stir to combine and add the pieces of confit. Continue simmering gently for 45 minutes, or until all the vegetables are tender.

❼ Preheat the oven to 400°F. If you wish, transfer the soup to an ovenproof tureen. Arrange the croutons over the top and sprinkle lightly with the grated cheese. Place on the top shelf of the oven and bake until the top is browned, about 10 minutes.

~·~·~·~·~·~·~·~·~·~

TO DRINK
A hearty red wine
from southwest
France.

~·~·~·~·~·~·~·~·~·~

BRUNSWICK CHICKEN SOUP

This soup-stew, which is thought to have originated in Virginia, was traditionally served at political rallys, family reunions and other large gatherings due to its variable and expandable nature. Early versions contained small game, and rabbit or game birds would be suitable substitutes for chicken if you wish to improvise.

SERVES 6

2 pounds chicken thighs or leg quarters
4–5 tablespoons dry white wine
6 cups chicken stock
2 carrots, sliced
large bouquet garni (parsley stems, thyme sprigs, celery leaves and bay leaf)
4 tablespoons butter
6 ounces button mushrooms, sliced

1 onion, finely chopped
1 garlic clove, minced
3 tablespoons flour
3 tomatoes, peeled, seeded and chopped
1 cup fresh or thawed frozen lima beans
1¼ cups corn kernels
salt and freshly ground pepper

❶ Put the chicken pieces, skin side down, in one layer in a large deep frying pan or flameproof casserole. Set over medium-high heat and cook until the chicken is evenly browned, turning once. Pour off all the rendered fat and add the wine. Cook for 1 minute and add the stock, stirring and scraping the bottom of the pan. Add the carrots and *bouquet garni*. Bring just to a boil, skimming off any foam as it rises to the surface. Reduce the heat to medium-low and simmer, partially covered, for 35–40 minutes until the chicken is tender, skimming from time to time.

❷ Using a slotted spoon, transfer the carrots and chicken pieces from the cooking liquid to a bowl. When the chicken is cool enough to handle, skin it and take the meat from the bones; discard the skin and bones. Cut the meat into small pieces and reserve with the carrots. Remove as much fat as possible from the cooking liquid and discard the *bouquet garni*.

❸ In a large saucepan or flameproof casserole, melt half the butter over medium-high heat. Add the mushrooms and cook, stirring frequently until golden. Transfer to the bowl with the carrots and chicken meat.

❹ Melt the remaining butter, add the onion and garlic, and cook, stirring frequently, over medium-low heat until just soft, about 5 minutes. Stir in the flour and cook for 2 minutes, stirring occasionally. Gradually pour in a third of the cooking liquid, whisking constantly. Bring to a boil, whisking, and cook for 2 minutes. Whisk in the remaining liquid until smooth. Add the tomatoes, lima beans and corn with the reserved chicken and vegetables. Bring back to a boil, reduce the heat to medium-low, and simmer until the beans are tender, about 20 minutes. Taste and adjust the seasoning and ladle into warm soup bowls.

~.~.~.~.~.~.~.~.~

TO DRINK
Fino Sherry

~.~.~.~.~.~.~.~.~

Seafood Soups

SOUPS CAPITALIZING ON THE BOUNTY OF THE SEA ARE UNIVERSAL. THEY MAY BE AN APPETITE TEMPTER OR THE MAINSTAY OF A MEAL, BUT WHEN YOU INHALE THE RISING STEAM LADEN WITH BRINEY AROMAS, YOU CAN ALMOST HEAR THE WAVES BREAKING. MODERN TRANSPORTATION ENSURES THAT EVEN INLAND AREAS ARE BLESSED WITH A RICH ARRAY OF FISH AND SHELLFISH – AND SEAFOOD SOUPS ARE AS GOOD FOR US AS THEY ARE TASTY.

SEAFOOD SOUPS

*A*ll countries with a coastline have a tradition of seafood soups and these vary enormously. Many were developed to utilize the diverse remains of unsold fish and shellfish from the day's catch and to make them go further. So, naturally, there is room for improvisation in this kind of soup.

Fish stock is the quickest of any to make and some shellfish, such as mollusks, make their own stock. Mussels and clams release a flavorful liquid during cooking which can, and should, be used in any soup from which they are made. Even the non-edible parts of some shellfish, such as the carapace, offer the makings of a tasty stock – so don't throw away those prawn or shrimp shells; boil them up.

Take care to avoid overcooking. Fish and shellfish are usually added towards the end of the cooking time of a soup, even though

Traditionally, fish soups vary with the catch. What is available determines what goes into the soup and the contents are likely to change from one time to the next. Most of the regional classics, such as Bouillabaisse, have local variations, particular to each village where it is made.

some parts may have been used in the initial preparation of the stock. Reheating fish soups is tricky. If you can't avoid it, strain out all the seafood and reheat the liquid, putting back the seafood just long enough to heat through.

The soups in this chapter offer a good way to enjoy all sorts of seafood. The more substantial soups, such as Bouillabaisse or Shrimp Gumbo, are traditionally served as a main course, perhaps with bread and a salad, and the estimated number of servings reflects this. If served as a starter, they are most appropriate before a relatively simple and light main course. Others, such as Creamy Mussel Soup, are normally served as a first course. Enjoy these soups when and as you like, adjusting the proportion of liquid to seafood – either more or less — to suit your preferences.

~.~.~.~.~.~.~.~.~.~

"This Bouillabaisse a noble dish is –
A sort of soup, or broth, or brew,
Or hotchpotch of all sorts of fishes,
That Greenwich never could outdo;
Green herbs, red peppers, mussels, saffron,
Soles, onions, garlic, roach, and dace;
All these to eat at Terré's tavern
In that one dish of Bouillabaisse."

"Ballad of Bouillabaiise"
W. M. Thackeray, 1811–63

~.~.~.~.~.~.~.~.~.~

71

PROVENCAL FISH SOUP

This rich soup, made from small rockfish and other essentially unsaleable fish, is found in virtually every restaurant along the Mediterranean coast – and it is usually wonderful. In Marseilles, pasta is added to the soup.

SERVES 6

2½ pounds small fish, gutted (use any sort except strong oily fish such as mackerel)
2 tablespoons olive oil
1 onion, halved and sliced
1 small fennel bulb, sliced
1½ pounds ripe tomatoes, cored and quartered, or 2½ cups canned chopped Italian tomatoes in juice
2 garlic cloves, sliced

bouquet garni (thyme sprigs, parsley stems and bay leaf)
zest of 1 orange (unwaxed or scrubbed), removed with a vegetable peeler
2 pinches saffron threads, dissolved in 2 tablespoons boiling water
3 cups water
TO SERVE
croutons (see page 122)
rouille (see page 124)

❶ Wash the fish under cold running water to remove any blood. Cut each fish into three or four pieces.
❷ Heat the olive oil in a large nonreactive saucepan or flameproof casserole. Add the onion and fennel, and cook over moderate heat, stirring occasionally, for 3–4 minutes, until the onion starts to soften.
❸ Add the fish, tomatoes, garlic, *bouquet garni*, orange zest, saffron and water. Reduce the heat and simmer, partially covered, for 30 minutes, stirring once or twice.
❹ Discard the *bouquet garni* and purée the fish and vegetable mixture in a food processor fitted with a steel blade, then work the mixture through the medium blade of a food mill or press through a sturdy strainer into the saucepan.
❺ Set the saucepan over medium heat, taste and adjust the seasoning, and simmer until the soup is heated through. Serve with croutons and *rouille*, if you wish.

~·~·~·~·~·~·~·~·~

VARIATION
Add 2 ounces broken
spaghetti or other small
pasta, cooked in boiling
salted water until tender,
after the soup has
been puréed.

~·~·~·~·~·~·~·~·~

CURRIED CRAB SOUP

Female crabs are best for soup because the roe adds flavor and color. This recipe, also known as She-crab Soup, is traditional in the South.

SERVES 4–6

5 tablespoons butter
1 shallot, finely chopped
4 tablespoons flour
½ teaspoon curry powder
2–3 tablespoons sherry
⅔ cup shellfish stock or bottled clam juice diluted with water
bay leaf

1¼ pounds tomatoes, peeled, seeded and chopped
1 cup light cream
½ pound crabmeat, picked over (about 1¾ cups)
Tabasco sauce (optional)
4–6 crab claws, cracked and peeled, for garnishing

❶ Melt the butter in a saucepan over medium-low heat. Add the shallot and cook for about 5 minutes until softened, stirring frequently. Stir in the flour and curry powder, and cook for 2 minutes. Add the sherry and cook, stirring constantly, until smooth and thick.
❷ Gradually stir in the stock and add the bay leaf and tomatoes. Simmer, stirring occasionally, for about 15 minutes, until the vegetables are soft.
❸ Work the soup through the medium blade of a food mill set over a bowl. (The soup may be prepared in advance up to this point. Leave to cool, cover and refrigerate. Reheat gently over low heat before continuing.)
❹ Stir in the cream and crabmeat. Taste and adjust the seasoning, and add a few drops of Tabasco sauce, if you wish. Ladle into warm bowls or a tureen and garnish with crab claws.

~·~·~·~·~·~·~·~·~

TO DRINK
A fruity, slightly
spicy medium-dry
white, such as
Gewürztraminer.

~·~·~·~·~·~·~·~·~

OYSTERS IN PARSLEY *and* GARLIC CREAM

The parsley in this creamy soup tames the garlic and gives it a brilliant color. It is delicious made with plump succulent oysters, but if you prefer, you can substitute cooked mussels or snails.

SERVES 4

16–20 oysters
1 large bunch of curly parsley, stems removed (about 6 cups leaves)
1½ cups whipping cream
1–2 garlic cloves, finely chopped
3–4 tablespoons shellfish stock or water (optional)
salt and freshly ground pepper
1 ripe tomato (preferably plum), peeled, seeded and diced

❶ Working over a bowl to catch the juices, open the oysters: hold in a cloth (flat-side up), push the knife into the hinge, then work it around until you can pry off the top shell. When all the oysters have been opened, strain the liquid through a strainer lined with damp cheesecloth. Remove the oysters from their shells and rinse under cold running water removing any bits of shell that adhere. Return the oysters to the filtered liquid. (This may be done several hours in advance; refrigerate, covered.)

❷ Bring a large saucepan of salted water to a boil. Drop in the parsley leaves and cook for 3–4 minutes until bright green and tender. Drain and refresh in cold water. Press with the back of a spoon to extract as much water as possible. (This may be done up to 1 day in advance.)

❸ Combine the cream and garlic in a medium saucepan and simmer over medium-low heat for 15 minutes until the garlic is tender and the cream has thickened slightly. Transfer to a blender or a food processor fitted with a steel blade, add the parsley and purée until smooth. Return the purée to the saucepan and stir in the oyster liquid. If you wish, thin with shellfish stock or water.

❹ Season to taste with salt, if needed, and pepper. Simmer the soup gently for about 5 minutes. Add the oysters and continue cooking for 1–2 minutes until the oysters are just heated through. Remove them with a slotted spoon and divide between four warm shallow soup plates. Ladle over the soup and garnish with diced tomato.

~.~.~.~.~.~.~.~.~.~

TO DRINK
A dry, slightly
sharp white, such as
Entre-Deux-Mers,
Muscadet or a North
American Semillon.

~.~.~.~.~.~.~.~.~.~

ITALIAN FISH SOUP

(Brodetto)

Like *bouillabaisse*, its counterpart in France, *brodetto* has innumerable variations. What distinguishes *brodetto* is braising the onions in vinegar for the soup base. Folklore dictates that 13 kinds of fish should be included, but unless you are feeding a crowd, this may not be practical. Use several kinds of firm white-fleshed fish and avoid particularly oily ones. According to tradition, the fish should not be too "noble" – this is the food of fishermen.

SERVES 6–8

2 tablespoons olive oil
2 onions, chopped
5 tablespoons white wine
    vinegar
2 garlic cloves, very finely
    chopped
1 carrot, grated
1 pound ripe tomatoes, peeled,
    seeded and chopped, or 1¾
    cups canned chopped Italian
    tomatoes in juice
2 cups dry white wine
2 tablespoons tomato purée
1½ cups fish stock, or 1 cup
    water

8 ounces squid, cleaned,
    skinned and cut into rings
grated zest of 1 lemon
    (unwaxed or scrubbed)
bay leaf
2 pounds white fish fillets, such
    as red snapper, cod,
    haddock, monkfish, shark or
    swordfish, skinned if wished
    and cut into pieces
1 pound small clams, scrubbed
2 tablespoons chopped fresh
    parsley
garlic croutons (see page 122)

❶ Heat the oil in a heavy nonreactive saucepan or flame-proof casserole over medium heat. Add the onions and cook until softened, about 3 minutes. Add the vinegar and cook, stirring frequently, until the vinegar has evaporated and continue cooking until the onions are golden.

❷ Add the garlic and carrot to the onion mixture, cook for 2–3 minutes and stir in the tomatoes and wine. Bring to a boil and boil for 1 minute. Stir in the tomato purée, stock or water and the squid, lemon zest and bay leaf. Reduce the heat to low and simmer, partially covered, until the squid is tender, about 30 minutes, stirring occasionally.

❸ Arrange the thicker pieces of fish over the mixture and push them into the soup. Put the thinner pieces of fish and the clams over the top, cover and continue simmering for about 5 minutes longer, or until the fish is opaque throughout and the clams have opened. Ladle into a warm tureen or bowls, sprinkle with parsley and serve with garlic croutons.

COOK'S TIP
The soup may be prepared several hours in advance except for adding the fish and shellfish. Allow to cool, cover and refrigerate. Reheat to simmering before continuing with step 3. If you wish, omit the squid and clams, and use only white fish, increasing the amount to about 2½ pounds.

TO DRINK
A crisp white country wine, such as Verdicchio or Frascati.

BLACK *and* WHITE SQUID SOUP

This soup has a spare, almost Oriental look, but the flavors are more Mediterranean. Black squid ink pasta is found in specialty shops featuring Italian products or in the gourmet sections of department stores and supermarkets. It doesn't taste particularly "fishy", so if you wish, substitute other small colored pasta shapes.

SERVES 4

12 ounces squid, cleaned, skinned and cut into thin rings
juice of 1 lemon
3 ounces squid ink pasta

4 cups fish or shellfish stock
pinch of saffron threads, soaked in 3 tablespoons boiling water
salt and white pepper

❶ Put the squid in a nonreactive saucepan with the lemon juice and water to cover generously. Bring to a boil, reduce the heat to low and simmer, partially covered, until the squid is tender, up to 1½ hours, adding more water if needed.

❷ Bring a moderately large saucepan of salted water to the boil, add the pasta and cook until tender but still a little chewy, *al dente*. Drain and rinse under cold running water.

❸ Bring the stock to a boil, strain in the saffron water and season with salt if needed and pepper to taste. Add the squid and pasta, and simmer for about 5 minutes until heated through. Ladle into a warm tureen or bowl.

~.~.~.~.~.~.~.~.~.~

COOK'S TIP
To clean squid, hold the sac-like body gently in one hand and the head in the other. Pull the head away from the body: the entrails should come with it. Rinse the sac under cold running water, loosen the transparent "bone" and pull it out. Gently squeeze out any remaining material inside the body and rinse again. Slice off the fins and slice the body into rings. Cut off and discard the part of the head above the tentacles containing the eyes and remove any hard central part.
Ready-cooked squid rings are sometimes available in fishmongers and supermarkets, and will save the time spent preparing and cooking the squid.

~·~·~·~·~·~·~·~·~

CREAMY MUSSEL SOUP

Variations of this soup are found all over France. This unadulterated version focuses on the briny flavor of the mussels. Sometimes saffron is added, as in Billi-Bi, the soup made famous at Maxime's in Paris, or other spices, such as the curry that is typical in Brittany.

SERVES 4

4½ pounds mussels
⅔ cup dry white wine
bouquet garni (thyme sprigs, parsley stems and bay leaf)
freshly ground pepper
1 tablespoon butter
2 large shallots, finely chopped

1 carrot, finely diced
1¼ cups whipping cream
1 tablespoon, dissolved in 2 tablespoons water
2 tablespoons chopped fresh parsley

❶ Discard any broken mussels and those with open shells that refuse to close when tapped. Under cold running water, scrape the mussel shells with a knife to remove any barnacles and pull out the stringy "beards". Rinse in several changes of cold water.

❷ In a large heavy saucepan or flameproof casserole combine the wine, *bouquet garni* and plenty of pepper. Bring to a boil over medium-high heat and cook for 2 minutes. Add the mussels, cover tightly and cook for about 5 minutes, or until the mussels open, shaking the pan occasionally. (Discard any that refuse to open.)

❸ When they are cool enough to handle, remove the mussels from the shells, straining any additional juices into the cooking liquid. Strain the cooking liquid through a strainer lined with damp cheesecloth.

❹ Melt the butter in a heavy saucepan. Add the shallots and carrot, and cook until the shallots are soft, stirring occasionally. Stir in the mussel cooking liquid and bring to a boil. Reduce the heat to low and simmer until the vegetables are tender, about 30 minutes.

❺ Add the cream and bring just to a boil. Stir the cornstarch mixture to combine, and stir it into the soup. Boil gently for 2–3 minutes until slightly thickened, stirring frequently. Add the mussels and cook for about 1–2 minutes longer to reheat them. Stir in the parsley and ladle into a warm tureen or soup bowls.

SMOKED SALMON CHOWDER

This rich, thick soup is full of flavor – a heartwarming lunch on a chilly day or an elegant, if substantial, starter. The poached salmon keeps it from being too salty and makes a tasty broth.

SERVES 6

1 tablespoon butter
3–4 shallots, finely chopped
2 celery stalks, finely chopped
5 cups water
1 bay leaf
2 salmon steaks (about 1 pound total weight)
2 potatoes (about 1 pound), diced

1¼ cups single cream
freshly ground pepper
7 ounces smoked salmon, cut in bite-sized pieces
1 tablespoon chopped fresh dill
1 tablespoon chopped fresh chives

❶ Melt the butter in a heavy nonreactive saucepan over medium-low heat. Add the shallots and celery, and sweat until slightly softened. Add the water and bay leaf, cover and simmer for 10 minutes.

❷ Add the salmon steaks and poach for 10 minutes over low heat, covered. Transfer to a plate and allow the fish to cool slightly. Discard the salmon skin and bones, and flake the flesh coarsely.

❸ Meanwhile, stir the potatoes into the cooking liquid and continue simmering for 15–20 minutes, partially covered, until they are tender.

❹ Add the cream to the chowder, season with pepper and simmer for about 5 minutes to heat through. Stir in the poached salmon, smoked salmon pieces and herbs, and continue cooking for 5 minutes. Taste and adjust the seasoning, and ladle into warm soup plates or bowls.

~.~.~.~.~.~.~.~.~.~

TO DRINK
A rich, lightly oaked
Chardonnay, or
perhaps a dry
Amontillado sherry.

~.~.~.~.~.~.~.~.~.~

SHELLFISH BISQUE

In Cajun cuisine, crayfish are typically used to make this soup, but virtually any kind of shellfish is suitable – small shrimp, crabs or lobsters, or use a mixture if you wish. Most of the flavor comes from the shells, so you could even make this soup after you have eaten the lobster!

SERVES 4

12 ounces small cooked shrimp in the shell, or 1 pound with heads, or about 1½ pounds hard-shelled shellfish, such as crabs, crayfish or lobster, cooked
2 tablespoons butter
4 tablespoons flour
2 tablespoons Cognac
cayenne pepper
4–5 tablespoons whipping cream
lemon juice

STOCK
2 teaspoons vegetable oil
shellfish shells and heads, or chopped small shellfish (about 1 pound)
1 onion, halved and sliced
1 small carrot, sliced
1 celery stalk, sliced
4 cups water
½ lemon (unwaxed or scrubbed), sliced
bouquet garni (thyme sprigs, parsley stems and bay leaf)

~.~.~.~.~.~.~.~.~

COOK'S TIP
If you have bought raw shellfish, cook it in boiling water and use the cooking water to make the stock. If using tiny crabs, the task of extracting any meat is too arduous, but chop them and cook as for shells.

~.~.~.~.~.~.~.~.~

❶ Remove the shells and heads, if any, from the shrimp, reserving them for the stock. For crab, crayfish or lobster, chop the shells in small pieces. Cover and chill the shellfish meat, either for use in the soup or for another purpose.

❷ For the stock, heat the oil in a large saucepan over high heat. Add the shellfish shells and heads, if any, and sauté until they start to brown. Reduce the heat to medium and add the onion, carrot and celery. Cook, stirring occasionally, for about 3 minutes, until the onion starts to soften. Add the water, lemon and *bouquet garni*. Bring to a boil, reduce the heat to low and simmer gently, partially covered, for 25 minutes. Strain the stock.

❸ Melt the butter in a heavy saucepan over moderate heat. Stir in the flour and cook until slightly golden, stirring occasionally. Add the Cognac and gradually pour in about half the stock, whisking vigorously until smooth, then add the remaining stock, still whisking. Season with cayenne pepper (salt is not usually needed). Reduce the heat, cover and simmer gently for about 5 minutes, stirring occasionally.

❹ Strain the soup if not completely smooth. Add the cream and lemon juice to taste. Reheat the shellfish meat, if using, briefly in the soup before serving.

~.~.~.~.~.~.~.~.~

TO DRINK
A rich, fruity dry white wine, such as Pinot Gris or Chardonnay, or dry fino sherry.

~.~.~.~.~.~.~.~.~

BRITTANY SEAFOOD SOUP

(Cotriade)

This creamy, French-style chowder is full of fish and shell-fish from the northern coastal waters. The sorrel gives it a pleasant piquancy, but if it is difficult to find, just omit it and add a squeeze of lemon juice. Alternatively, stir a tea-spoonful of curry powder into the cream before adding, as this is also typical in Brittany. Breton ports played an important role in the spice trade and such spices are not unusual in the regional cuisine.

SERVES 8

2 pounds mussels, scrubbed
   and debearded
6 tablespoons dry cider or
   white wine
freshly ground pepper
2 tablespoons butter
2 leeks, thinly sliced
1 large onion, finely chopped
1 pound potatoes, diced
5 cups fish stock
bouquet garni (thyme sprigs,
   parsley stems and bay leaf)
5 ounces fresh sorrel leaves,

washed and blotted dry
1½ pounds white fish fillets,
   such as cod, turbot and
   monkfish, skinned and cut
   into large bite-sized pieces
12 ounces cooked or raw
   medium shrimp, peeled
12 ounces small scallops
1 cup whipping cream or crème
   fraîche
large croutons, for serving
   (see page 122)

❶ Put the mussels into a large heavy saucepan with the cider or wine and a little pepper. Steam, tightly covered, over high heat until the shells open, about 5 minutes (discard any that refuse to open). When cool enough to handle, remove the mussels from the shells. Strain the cooking liquid through damp cheesecloth.

❷ Melt half the butter in a flameproof casserole over medium-low heat. Cook the leeks and onion until the onion starts to soften, about 3 minutes. Stir in the potatoes, stock and strained mussel liquid. Bring to a boil, add the *bouquet garni* and reduce the heat to medium-low. Simmer, partially covered, until the potatoes are tender, about 20 minutes.

❸ Melt the remaining butter in a small frying pan or sauce-pan over low heat. Add the sorrel, stir until it is wilted and remove from the heat.

❹ Add the fish to the soup, starting with the thickest pieces and putting in the thinner ones after 1–2 minutes. A few minutes after all the fish has been added, add the shrimp, scallops and mussels, and continue simmering gently for 2–3 minutes until all the seafood is cooked (the flesh is opaque throughout). Using a slotted spoon, transfer the fish and shellfish to a warm tureen and cover to keep warm.

❺ Bring the soup to the boil and stir in the cream and the sorrel. Continue boiling gently, stirring occasionally, for 4–5 minutes until slightly reduced and thickened. Taste for sea-soning and ladle the soup over the fish and shellfish. Serve with croutons, if you wish.

CLAM CHILI

Clams are often underrated, but they are wonderfully versatile. This "chili" is thick and spicy, and the meaty texture of the clams gives it body and brings an aromatic marine element that makes it quite unusual.

SERVES 6–8

¾ cup (7 ounces) dried black
    beans or navy beans, soaked
    overnight in cold water to
    cover generously, or one 14-
    ounce can black or
    cannellini beans, rinsed
½ cup dry white wine
4 pounds small or medium-
    sized clams, scrubbed, or
    two 10-ounce cans baby
    clams, drained, plus
    1½ cups bottled clam juice
2 tablespoons olive oil
2 onions, finely chopped
1 large carrot, finely chopped
1 celery stalk, finely chopped
1 red or yellow bell pepper,
    seeded and finely chopped
3–4 garlic cloves, minced

1–2 roasted ancho or jalapeño
    chilies, finely chopped
4 ounces chorizo or pepperoni,
    finely diced
1½ pounds tomatoes, peeled,
    seeded and chopped, or one
    14-ounce can chopped
    Italian tomatoes in juice
1½ cups tomato juice or
    tomato-clam juice
2 tablespoons tomato paste
2 teaspoons chili powder, or to
    taste
bay leaf
¼ teaspoon each dried thyme
    and oregano
3–4 tablespoons finely chopped
    cilantro or parsley

❶ If using dried beans, drain them, put into a saucepan with cold water to cover and set over high heat. Bring to a boil and boil for 10 minutes. Drain and add fresh cold water to cover. Bring to a boil again, reduce the heat to low and simmer until the beans are tender, 1½–2 hours.

❷ In a large heavy saucepan or flameproof casserole combine the clams and wine. Cover tightly, set over medium-high heat and cook for 2–4 minutes, or until they open, shaking the pan occasionally.

❸ Heat the oil in a large heavy saucepan or flameproof casserole over medium heat. Add the onions and cook for 5 minutes, stirring frequently. Add the carrot, celery and pepper, cover and continue cooking until the vegetables are tender, abut 3 minutes more, stirring occasionally. Stir in the garlic, chilies, chorizo or pepperoni, tomatoes, tomato juice and clam cooking liquid, or if using canned clams, add the wine and clam juice, and bring to the boil.

❹ Drain the beans, reserving the cooking liquid if using dried beans. Add the beans to the soup, reduce the heat to low and simmer very gently, stirring occasionally, until the vegetables are tender and the soup is thick, about 45 minutes. If you like a thinner soup, add as much of the bean cooking liquid or water as you wish.

❺ Taste and adjust the seasoning. Stir in the clams and heat through. Ladle into a warm tureen or bowls and sprinkle with cilantro or parsley.

SHRIMP GUMBO

Gumbo is a Cajun creation with almost infinite variations. Many but not all versions contain okra, the vegetable that gives this soup its name, and the soup may be seasoned with *filé*, made from ground sassafras leaves. Most versions start with a brown *roux*, one of the hallmarks of Cajun cooking. Feel free to make substitutions – the Acadians, or Cajuns, as they became known, have long been recognized for their inventive use of available ingredients.

SERVES 6–8

2 tablespoons olive oil
1 pound spicy sausage, cut into
   ¾-inch pieces
3 ounces smoked country ham
   or prosciutto, diced
4 tablespoons flour
2 onions, finely chopped
1 small green bell pepper,
   seeded and finely chopped
2 celery stalks, finely chopped
3–4 garlic cloves, very finely
   chopped
3–4 scallions, finely chopped

1¼ pounds tomatoes, peeled,
   seeded and chopped (about
   2½ cups)
2 cups water
bay leaf
¼ teaspoon gumbo filé
   (optional)
1 pound okra, trimmed and cut
   into ¼-inch pieces
2–3 cups shellfish or chicken
   stock, or more water
1 pound cooked shelled medium
   shrimp, deveined
hot cooked rice, for serving

~.~.~.~.~.~.~.~.~.~

COOK'S TIP
For maximum flavor,
buy shrimp in the
shell, peel and
devein them, and
make shellfish stock
with the shells.

~·~·~·~·~·~·~·~·~

❶ Heat the oil in a Dutch oven or heavy flameproof casserole over a medium heat. Add the sausage and cook until lightly browned, then add the ham or prosciutto and continue cooking until both are browned. Remove with a slotted spoon and drain on paper towels.

❷ Pour out all but 2 tablespoons of the fat in the pan and sprinkle over the flour. Stir constantly until it darkens to a medium brown, about the color of peanut butter. Stir in the onion and pepper, and cook for 2–3 minutes until they start to soften. Add the celery, garlic and scallions, and continue cooking for 2 minutes longer, stirring occasionally.

❸ Stir in the tomatoes and water. Bring to a boil and add the bay leaf and gumbo *filé*, if using, and the sausage and ham. Reduce the heat to medium-low and simmer for 30 minutes.

❹ Bring a large saucepan of salted water to a boil, add the okra and boil for 4 minutes. Refresh in cold running water and drain well.

❺ Add the okra to the soup with 2 cups stock or water and simmer for 15–20 minutes until the okra is tender, stirring occasionally. Thin with more stock or water, if you wish, bring to a simmer and add the shrimp. Simmer until heated through, about 5 minutes. Transfer to a warm tureen and serve with rice, or put a little rice in the bottom of warm bowls and ladle over the gumbo.

~.~.~.~.~.~.~.~.~.~

TO DRINK
A robust, spicy
red wine.

~·~·~·~·~·~·~·~·~

MEDITERRANEAN FISH SOUP

(Bouillabaisse)

All along the Mediterranean coast, from Italy to Spain, variations of this soup abound. Almost any combination of fish and shellfish can be used, as this kind of soup was originally made from anything the fishermen had left from their catch, but strong-flavored oily fish are best avoided. A flavorful fish stock is essential, so ask the fishmonger for the heads, tails and trimmings from the fish fillets, plus extra if available.

SERVES 8

3 pounds firm white fish fillets, such as sea bass, snapper and monkfish
3 tablespoons olive oil
grated zest of 1 orange (unwaxed or scrubbed)
1 garlic clove, minced
pinch saffron threads
2 tablespoons Pernod (anise liquor)
1½ pounds large shrimp
1 small fennel bulb, finely chopped
1 large onion, finely chopped
8 ounces small new potatoes, sliced
12 ounces sea scallops, rinsed
croutons (see page 122)
rouille (see page 124)

STOCK
2–3 pounds fish heads, bones and trimmings
2 tablespoons olive oil
2 leeks, sliced
1 onion, halved and sliced
1 red bell pepper, cored and sliced
1½ pounds ripe tomatoes, cored and quartered
4 garlic cloves, sliced
bouquet garni (thyme sprigs, parsley stems and bay leaf)
zest of 1 orange (unwaxed or scrubbed), removed with a vegetable peeler
2–3 pinches saffron threads
8 cups water

~.~.~.~.~.~.~.~.~

COOK'S TIP
You can prepare the
rouille and croutons in
advance and make
the stock for the soup
early in the day while
the fish fillets
marinate. Then the
final assembly isn't
too difficult.

~·~·~·~·~·~·~·~·~

❶ Cut the fish fillets in small serving pieces. Trim off any thin ragged bits and reserve for the stock. Put the fish in a bowl with 2 tablespoons of the olive oil, the orange zest, garlic, saffron and Pernod. Turn to coat well. Peel the shrimp and reserve the shells. Cover and refrigerate the shrimp and the fish separately.

❷ For the stock, rinse the fish heads, bones and trimmings under cold running water to remove any blood. Heat the olive oil in a large nonreactive saucepan or flameproof casserole. Add the leeks, onion and pepper, and cook over medium heat, stirring occasionally, until the onion starts to soften, about 5 minutes. Add the reserved shrimp shells, fish heads, bones and trimmings, and continue cooking for 2 minutes. Stir in the tomatoes, garlic, *bouquet garni*, orange zest, saffron and water (top up if necessary to cover ingredients). Bring to a boil, skimming off the foam as it rises, then reduce the heat and simmer, covered, for 30 minutes, skimming once or twice. Strain the stock.

❸ To finish the soup, heat the remaining tablespoon of olive oil in a deep sauté pan or wide flameproof casserole over medium heat. Cook the chopped fennel and onion until the onion starts to soften, about 5 minutes, then add the strained stock. Bring to a boil, add the potatoes and cook for 5 minutes. Reduce the heat to medium-low and add the fish, starting with the thickest pieces and putting in the thinner ones after 2–3 minutes. Add the shrimp and scallops, and continue simmering gently until all the seafood is cooked (opaque throughout). Transfer the fish, shellfish and potatoes to a warm tureen or soup plates. Taste for seasoning and ladle the soup over. Serve with croutons spread with *rouille*.

~.~.~.~.~.~.~.~.~

TO DRINK
A Côtes de Provence
white or rosé or
white Cassis.

~·~·~·~·~·~·~·~·~

MUSSEL *and* NEW POTATO SOUP

This light but satisfying, unusual mussel soup is full of contrasting colors and complementary flavors. It is inspired by a dish created by a Michelin-starred chef in Burgundy.

SERVES 4–6

4½ pounds mussels
4 cups water
8–10 garlic cloves, unpeeled (about ½ large head)
3 thyme sprigs, or ¼ teaspoon dried thyme
3 marjoram sprigs, or ¼ teaspoon dried marjoram
bay leaf

pinch of saffron
10 ounces long thin waxy potatoes, peeled and thinly sliced
2 plum tomatoes, peeled, seeded and finely diced
1 cup spinach leaves (about 1 ounce) cut in thin ribbons
aïoli, for serving (see page 84)

❶ Discard any broken mussels and those with open shells that refuse to close when tapped. Under cold running water, scrape the mussel shells with a knife to remove any barnacles and pull out the stringy "beards." Rinse in several changes of cold water.

❷ Put the mussels in a large heavy saucepan or flameproof casserole and cook, tightly covered, over high heat for 4–6 minutes until the shells open, shaking the pan occasionally (discard any that refuse to open). When cool enough to handle, remove the mussels from the shells. Strain the cooking liquid through a strainer lined with damp cheesecloth and reserve.

❸ Combine the water, garlic, thyme, marjoram, bay leaf and saffron in a saucepan. Bring to a boil over high heat, reduce the heat to medium and simmer, partially covered, for 30 minutes.

❹ Strain the herb and garlic infusion, and combine with the mussel cooking liquid. Add the potatoes and set over medium-low heat. Bring to a simmer and cook until the potatoes are tender, about 15 minutes. Add the tomatoes, spinach and mussels, and cook until the mussels are heated through. Ladle into a warm tureen or individual bowls and serve with *aïoli*, if you wish.

ORIENTAL SCALLOP SOUP

This exotic soup is quick and easy to prepare. Miso, used as a base for many different soups in Japan, is made from soya beans blended with other ingredients, such as barley (*mugi miso*), brown rice (*genmai miso*) or sweet rice (*shiro miso*), and fermented to develop a unique flavor. Miso made purely from soya beans (*hatcho miso*) has a stronger taste.

SERVES 4

4 cups water
4 teaspoons miso (bean paste, available at health food shops)
3 ounces shiitake mushrooms, stems removed
1 garlic clove, halved
1-inch piece lemon grass or peeled fresh gingerroot

3–4 scallions, cut in julienne strips about 2 inches long
1 teaspoon light soy sauce, or to taste
1 teaspoon lemon juice, or to taste
6 large sea scallops, about 8 ounces
cilantro leaves, for garnishing

❶ Bring the water to a boil in a medium saucepan. Thin the miso with a little of the water, reduce the heat to low and stir in the diluted miso.

❷ Slice the mushrooms thinly and add to the miso broth with the garlic and lemon grass or ginger. Simmer gently for 10–12 minutes, or until the mushrooms are tender. Remove the garlic and lemon grass or ginger, and stir in the scallion strips. Season with soy sauce and lemon juice.

❸ Pull off the coral, if any, carefully. Discard the small hard muscle on the side and slice the scallops crosswise to form two or three thinner rounds from each. Simmer the scallops and corals in the broth until the flesh becomes opaque, 1–2 minutes.

❹ Divide the scallop rounds between four warm bowls (white if possible), ladle the soup over and float a few cilantro leaves on each serving.

~·~·~·~·~·~·~·~·~

COOK'S TIP
If you like a more fishy flavor, stir in a small amount of Oriental fish sauce or anchovy paste before serving.

GARLIC FISH SOUP

(Bourride)

Although many of the ingredients are the same, this soup looks nothing like its "cousin" *bouillabaisse* and, in fact, fishmongers in the Mediterranean region sell different fish for these two soups. Smooth and white, bourride gets its creamy texture and powerful flavor from *aïoli*, a pungent garlic mayonnaise much used in Provence, which, combined with egg yolks, is used to thicken the soup. The fish is sometimes served apart from the soup. If you prefer, omit the egg yolks to thicken the soup and just stir the remaining half of the *aïoli* into the soup until combined for an equally tasty but thinner soup.

SERVES 6

5 cups fish stock or water
½ cup dry white wine
1 onion, chopped
1 leek sliced
zest of ½ orange (unwaxed or scrubbed), removed with a vegetable peeler
generous pinch of fennel seeds
2 teaspoons tomato paste
large bouquet garni (thyme sprigs, parsley stems, leek greens and bay leaf)
2½ pounds firm white fish fillets or steaks, such as monkfish or turbot

3 egg yolks
2 tablespoons crème fraîche or whipping cream
salt and white pepper
croutons, for serving (see page 122)
AIOLI
3–4 garlic cloves, very finely chopped
1 egg yolk, at room temperature
salt
¾ cup extra-virgin olive oil, at room temperature
juice of 1 large lemon

❶ For the *aïoli*, combine the garlic, egg yolk and a pinch of salt in a food processor fitted with a steel blade and process for 1 minute. Add the oil by drops until the mixture begins to thicken, then add the remaining oil in a thin stream. Add the lemon juice and pulse to combine. Remove about half of the *aïoli* and reserve for serving; leave the remainder in the container. (Alternatively, if making in advance, refrigerate, covered.)

❷ Combine the stock, wine, onion, leek, orange zest, fennel seeds and tomato paste in a large saucepan or flame-proof casserole. Bring to a boil, reduce the heat to medium-low and simmer for 10 minutes. Add the fish, starting with the thickest pieces and putting in the thinner ones after 1–2 minutes. Continue simmering gently for about 5 minutes until all the fish is cooked (the flesh is opaque throughout). Using a slotted spoon, transfer the fish to a warm tureen and cover to keep warm. Strain the cooking liquid, rinse the saucepan and return the liquid to it.

❸ Add the egg yolks to the *aïoli* in the food processor and pulse to combine. Pour in 2–3 ladlefuls of the cooking liquid and process until combined. Pour back into the saucepan, add the *crème fraîche* or cream and stir constantly over low heat until the mixture thickens slightly, about 5 minutes. (Do not allow it to boil.) Taste and adjust the seasoning, adding salt, if needed, and white pepper. Ladle over the fish, serve with croutons and the remaining *aïoli*, if you like.

~.~.~.~.~.~.~.~.~.~

To Drink
A robust white wine
from the region, such
as Côtes du Lubéron.

~.~.~.~.~.~.~.~.~.~

CIOPPINO

This soup, associated with San Francisco's North Beach area, is probably derived from the Italian seafood soup, *ciuppin*. As with most seafood soups, the ingredients can be varied. This version, which uses only shellfish, calls for mussels, squid and prawns, but clams, scallops, crab claws or small lobsters may be added or substituted. Be sure to include either mussels or clams for their flavorful liquid.

SERVES 4–6

1 pound mussels, scrubbed and debearded
1 tablespoon olive oil
1 large onion, finely chopped
½ fennel bulb, finely chopped
1½ pounds tomatoes, peeled, seeded and chopped
2 garlic cloves, very finely chopped
1¼ cups dry white wine

1 cup tomato juice
½ cup water
8 ounces cleaned squid, cut in thin rings, boiled until tender
bay leaf
12 ounces cooked shelled medium shrimp, deveined
3 tablespoons chopped fresh parsley

❶ Put the mussels into a large heavy saucepan or flame-proof casserole and cook, tightly covered, over high heat for 4–6 minutes until the shells open, shaking the pan occasionally. Remove the mussels and discard any that refuse to open. Strain the cooking liquid through a strainer lined with damp cheesecloth and reserve. When the mussels are cool enough to handle, set aside a few in the shells for garnishing, one or two per serving. Remove the remainder of the mussels from the shells and strain any additional juices into the cooking liquid.

❷ Heat the olive oil in a heavy saucepan over medium-low heat. Add the onion and fennel, and cook for 2–3 minutes, until just softened, stirring occasionally. Stir in the tomatoes and garlic, and continue cooking for 10 minutes. Add the wine and bring to a boil, then add the tomato juice, water, reserved mussel cooking liquid, squid and bay leaf. Reduce the heat to low and simmer until the vegetables and squid are tender, about 20 minutes.

❸ Stir in the shrimp and shelled mussels, and simmer over medium-low until heated through. Remove the bay leaf, ladle into a warm tureen or bowls and sprinkle with parsley. Garnish with the reserved whole mussels.

~·~·~·~·~·~·~·~·~·~·~

TO DRINK
A very dry white,
such as a Californian
Fumé Blanc.

~·~·~·~·~·~·~·~·~·~·~

CHAPTER FIVE

Fruit Soups

RUIT IS ONE OF THE JEWELS OF THE TABLE AND ITS VERSATILITY MERITS EXPERIMENTATION. FRUIT SOUPS PROVIDE THE PERFECT OPPORTUNITY. THEY MAY BE COOLING OR STIMULATING, RICH OR ETHEREAL, UNCTUOUS IN TEXTURE OR CHUNKY. THEY MAY BE SERVED TO BEGIN A MEAL OR TO END IT – EITHER WAY, THEY MAKE IT MEMORABLE. THIS SELECTION OF FRUIT SOUPS CAN OPEN THE DOOR TO A COLORFUL WORLD OF CREATIVITY.

FRUIT SOUPS

*W*e often think of soups as essentially savory, but a dessert soup or a semi-sweet soup served as a first course, can hold great appeal. Fruit soups are satisfying in many ways. They are unusual, and perfect to start or follow a substantial main course.

On a warm day, why not begin a meal with Minted Melon Soup, to revive flagging appetites with its cooling effect? Or serve a wine-based fruit soup, such as California Iced Fruit Soup – a prelude as refreshing as a fruit punch – and much more memorable.

Fruit soup is often uncooked to retain the natural flavors. In its simplest form, it consists of puréed fruit combined with some other ingredient to enhance its flavor. The fruit may need to be heated briefly to make it juicier. These uncooked fruit soups should be consumed within a day. Those that contain cooked ingredients keep longer. Most fruit soups are not thickened in the way that savory soups might be, and flour or starch is almost never used. If puréed, the fruit itself becomes the thickening agent, or it may be

Fruit soups offer such color and variety – a rainbow of bright sunny hues or cooling pastels. They are refreshing, intriguing and a little unexpected. When you use fruit at its peak of ripeness, the soup captures the essence of melons, peaches or plums.

88

~.~.~.~.~.~.~.~.~.~

"Ripe Apples drop about my head,
The Luscious Clusters of the Vine
Upon my mouth do crush their Wine;
The Nectaren, and curious Peach,
Into my hands themselves do reach;
Stumbling on Melons, as I pass."

THE GARDEN
Andrew Marvell, 1621–78

~˙~˙~˙~˙~˙~˙~˙~˙~˙~

Eternally popular citrus adds a refreshing tang to fruit soups, whether playing a major or minor role, while exotic fruits, such as papaya, pomegranates and mango, or musky-scented melon, bring their tantalizing highly perfumed flavors.

combined with cream, yogurt or custard to achieve a smooth, luscious texture.

Many fruit soups have wine among the main ingredients. This can help to establish the balance of sweet and acidic elements, particularly with ripe berries and other red fruits.

Fruit soups lend themselves to dramatic serving presentations. The colors themselves provide part of the dramatic element – most of these soups are jewel-like. But there is also the potential for originality in serving, such as decorating the side of the bowl – or the plate under it if using glass – with fresh flowers or serving from an ice bowl in which fruit and flowers are frozen.

SUMMER BERRY SOUP

Croutons in a sweet soup? The combination of the fruit-soaked "croutons" atop luscious juicy berries rising from a pool of red berry purée provides a real dose of summer flavor.

SERVES 4

1 pound ripe mixed berries
 (raspberries, blackberries,
 small strawberries,
 blueberries and black
 currants), hulled
 or stemmed if necessary
4 tablespoons soft light brown
 sugar, or to taste

8 slices firm white bread
 or brioche
6 tablespoons whipping cream
additional berries and mint
 leaves, to decorate
RASPBERRY PUREE
12 ounces ripe raspberries
6 tablespoons confectioners'
 sugar, or to taste

❶ Combine the mixed berries and brown sugar in a non-reactive saucepan and set over medium-low heat until the juices start to run, about 3–4 minutes. (The fruit should not be completely cooked.) Remove from the heat and leave to cool slightly. Strain the fruit, without pressing down on it, and reserve the juice in a large bowl.

❷ Line the bottom of four ramekins (about ¾ cup capacity) with rounds of wax paper. Cut eight rounds from the bread the same diameter as the ramekins. Dip four of the bread rounds in the reserved juice and place in the bottom of the ramekins.

❸ Divide the fruit among the ramekins, pressing it down gently. Dip the remaining bread rounds in the reserved juice and place on top of the fruit. Cover the ramekins tightly and refrigerate for at least 3 hours or overnight.

❹ For the raspberry purée, put the raspberries in a food processor fitted with a steel blade and process until smooth, then press through a strainer. Alternatively, work the berries through the fine blade of a food mill. Add the purée to the reserved juices from the fruit and add the confectioners' sugar, plus more if you wish, and stir until it has dissolved. Cover and refrigerate until cold.

❺ To serve, unmold the ramekins into chilled shallow bowls and remove the paper. Pour the raspberry purée around them and drizzle the cream into the purée. Place a few berries on the top of each serving with mint leaves to decorate.

APRICOT SOUP

This bright, colorful dessert tastes of summer sunshine, even in winter. Using two kinds of apricots intensifies the flavor and you can make the purées up to one day ahead for easy assembly just before serving.

SERVES 6

4 ounces dried apricots
1 cup orange juice, plus more if needed
1 pound fresh apricots, halved and stoned
4 tablespoons sweet white wine
1–2 tablespoons sugar
2 tablespoons apricot or peach liqueur
⅔ cup crème fraîche or sour cream

❶ Combine the dried apricots and orange juice in a small nonreactive saucepan. Set over medium-low heat and simmer, covered, until the apricots are tender, about 35 minutes. Set aside to cool.

❷ Combine the fresh apricots, wine and sugar to taste in a medium-sized nonreactive saucepan and bring to a boil. Reduce the heat and simmer until the fruit is very tender, about 25 minutes. Transfer the fruit to a food processor fitted with a steel blade and process until smooth, then press through a strainer into a bowl. Stir in the liqueur and refrigerate until cold.

❸ Scrape the dried apricot mixture into the food processor and process until smooth. Add the cream and pulse just until combined. The mixture should be about the same consistency as the cooked fresh apricots; add more orange juice if necessary. Transfer to a bowl and refrigerate until cold.

❹ To serve, divide the fresh apricot mixture between chilled bowls and put a large spoonful of the dried apricot and cream mixture in the center, dividing it evenly. Using the handle of a small spoon or a skewer, draw the dried apricot mixture out towards the edge of the bowl in five or six places to make a starburst pattern, curving at the outer edges, if you wish.

CALIFORNIAN ICED FRUIT SOUP

This wine-based fruit soup is spectacular served in a fruit and flower ice bowl. You can make the decorative ice bowl several days in advance for convenience. Set it on a water-proof tray or a deep platter and surround with more flowers and leaves before filling with the fruit soup. The fresh fruit used in the soup can be varied according to seasonal availability.

SERVES 6

3 cups fruity white California wine
½ cup sugar, plus more if needed
2 lemons (unwaxed or scrubbed)
3 oranges (unwaxed or scrubbed)
2 ripe peaches, peeled and sliced, preferably white-fleshed
1½ cups strawberries, halved if large
1 cup blueberries or other small berries
decorative ice bowl, for serving (see page 121)

❶ Combine the wine and sugar in a glass or ceramic bowl. Stir to dissolve.

❷ Slice the lemons and one of the oranges thinly. Add them to the wine mixture and chill for several hours, stirring and pressing on the fruit occasionally.

❸ Peel and segment the remaining oranges over a bowl to catch the juice. Add the peaches, strawberries and blueberries, and stir to coat the fruit with orange juice. Taste and add sugar if needed. Cover and refrigerate until serving.

❹ Strain the wine mixture into a serving bowl made of ice (or a glass serving bowl) and stir in the fruit and accumulated juices. Serve immediately.

STRAWBERRY SOUP

At the height of the strawberry season, celebrate their perfection with this soup. If your berries are honey-sweet, you may not need any sugar!

SERVES 6

1½ pounds strawberries, hulled
juice of 1 lemon
4 tablespoons sugar,
or to taste
2 cups freshly squeezed,
strained orange juice (about
4 oranges)

3 tablespoons Cointreau or
Kirsch
½ cup whipping cream
mint sprigs or strawberry
leaves, for decorating

❶ Reserve 6 berries to decorate and put the remainder in a food processor fitted with a steel blade or in a blender. Add the lemon juice and sugar, depending on the sweetness of the berries and your taste, and purée until smooth.

❷ Strain the purée into a bowl and stir in the orange juice and Cointreau or Kirsch. Cover and refrigerate until cold.

❸ Whip the cream until it forms soft peaks. Ladle the soup into chilled shallow bowls, preferably glass, and top each serving with a dollop of whipped cream. Decorate with the reserved berries and mint sprigs or strawberry leaves.

SUNSET FRUIT SOUP

Intensely colored exotic fruit purées arranged in adjoining bands make a dramatic presentation. Shallow glass soup plates or other very shallow plain dishes are most effective for serving this soup.

SERVES 6–8

¼ cup sugar
¼ cup water
1 small pineapple, peeled and
cored, about 12 ounces
7 tablespoons lime juice

1 large mango, about
1 pound
1 large papaya, about
¾ pound

❶ Combine the sugar and water in a small saucepan and bring to a boil, stirring occasionally. Remove from the heat and let the syrup cool.

❷ Cut the pineapple into chunks and put in a food processor fitted with a steel blade with 1 tablespoon of the lime juice and 3 tablespoons of the sugar syrup. Purée until smooth. Scrape into a small bowl, cover and refrigerate.

❸ Peel the mango. Cut down each side of the center stone and put the flesh in the food processor (no need to wash it between puréeing each fruit), then cut off all the flesh adhering to the stone and add it to the workbowl. Add 3 tablespoons of the lime juice and 2 tablespoons of the sugar syrup and purée until smooth. Scrape into a small bowl, cover and refrigerate.

❹ Halve the papaya and discard the seeds. Scoop the flesh into the food processor, leaving virtually none remaining on the skin. Add the remaining lime juice and sugar syrup and purée until smooth. Scrape into a small bowl, cover and refrigerate.

❺ To serve, arrange the fruit purées in chilled shallow bowls or dishes in adjoining bands from lightest to darkest colors.

~.~.~.~.~.~.~.~.~.~

VARIATION
If any one of the
fruits is unavailable,
substitute yellow-
or orange-fleshed
melon.

~.~.~.~.~.~.~.~.~.~

RUBY PLUM SOUP

This rich red soup is reminiscent of mulled wine, but with a pleasing fruity element. Using plums with red rather than yellow flesh will give the best color. In frosty weather you could serve it hot, if you wish, in punch cups with a cinnamon stick in each.

SERVES 8

2½ pounds ripe red plums,
*   halved and pitted*
¾ cup water
grated zest of 1 lemon
*   (unwaxed or scrubbed)*
3–4 allspice berries
5–6 cloves

5–6 peppercorns
2½ cups ruby port
1–2 tablespoons runny honey
1 cinnamon stick
6–8 tablespoons whipping
*   cream, for decorating*

❶ Put the plums in a heavy saucepan with the water, lemon zest, allspice berries, cloves and peppercorns. Set over medium-low heat, cover and cook gently for about 20 minutes, or until the plums are very tender.

❷ Work the plums through the fine blade of a food mill set over a clean saucepan or press the mixture through a strainer. Discard the spices.

❸ Stir in the port and honey to taste, add the cinnamon stick and bring to the boil. Reduce the heat to low and simmer for 15 minutes, stirring occasionally. Let cool, remove the cinnamon stick, cover and refrigerate until cold.

❹ Ladle the soup into chilled bowls and drizzle two vertical lines of cream over the top of each serving. Using a toothpick or thin skewer, draw crosswise through the cream a little way into the soup, first in one direction, then in the other, wiping the stick between, to make a feather-like design. Alternatively, just drizzle the cream in random lines to decorate.

MINTED MELON SOUP

There is nothing more refreshing than melon – it is light and cool, and prepared this way, it makes a pretty pastel picture. Only ripe melons will do for this cold soup, in fact the melon purée can be made from slightly overripe melons. Use whatever varieties of melons are available, as long as they are different colors. Serve this soup either as a starter or dessert.

SERVES 4

1 large ripe green-fleshed melon, such as Honeydew, Galia or Ogen, about 2 pounds
5–6 mint leaves, plus more to decorate
⅔ cup medium Muscat wine or white port
½ cup water
1–2 tablespoons lime juice (optional)
2–3 tablespoons caster sugar
½ large ripe orange-fleshed melon, such as Cantaloup, Charentais or Casaba, about 1 pound

❶ Discard the seeds from the green-fleshed melon and scoop the flesh into a blender or a food processor fitted with a steel blade. Add the mint, wine, water, lime juice, if using, and sugar. Purée until smooth and refrigerate, covered.
❷ Discard the seeds of the orange-fleshed melon and, using a melon ball cutter, scoop out the flesh in small balls, or cut into cubes. Cover and refrigerate.
❸ To serve, divide the melon purée among four chilled bowls. Arrange the melon balls on top, dividing them evenly, and decorate with mint.

~.~.~.~.~.~.~.~.~.~

COOK'S TIP
If you wish, use two smaller green-fleshed melons instead of 1 large one and serve the soup from the melon halves, cutting them in half to form zig-zag edge for a more decorative effect. Try to find oval melons and cut them through the stem end instead of through the "equator," so the containers are as shallow as possible – otherwise the melon balls will be submerged.

~.~.~.~.~.~.~.~.~.~

CITRUS SOUP

The richness of the smooth custard is a perfect background for the pleasantly sharp citrus fruit.

SERVES 4

1 vanilla bean
1¼ cups whole milk
1 egg
2 egg yolks
5 tablespoons sugar
1 tablespoon Cointreau, or other orange liqueur
2 large seedless oranges (unwaxed or scrubbed)
1 ruby grapefruit

❶ Put the vanilla bean and milk in a medium saucepan and bring just to a boil over medium-high heat, stirring frequently. Remove from the heat and cover. Allow to stand for 15–20 minutes and remove the vanilla bean.
❷ In a medium bowl, whisk the egg, egg yolks and 2 tablespoons of the sugar for 2–3 minutes until thick and creamy. Whisk in the hot milk and return the mixture to the saucepan. With a wooden spoon, stir over medium-low heat until the custard begins to thicken and coat the back of the spoon (do not allow it to boil or the custard may curdle). Immediately strain into a cold bowl set in a larger bowl of ice water and allow to cool, stirring occasionally. Stir in the Cointreau and refrigerate, covered.
❸ With a vegetable peeler, remove the zest from one of the oranges in wide strips. Stack two or three strips at a time and slice into very thin matchstick slivers. Combine the remaining sugar and 5 tablespoons of water in a small saucepan and bring to a boil, stirring occasionally. Add the orange zest, reduce the heat to low and simmer for 10 minutes. Remove from the heat and allow to cool.
❹ Peel the oranges and grapefruit, working over a bowl to catch the juices, and segment the fruit by cutting between the membranes. Add 3–4 tablespoons of the juice to the custard.
❺ Divide the custard among four chilled shallow bowls. Arrange the fruit in a starburst pattern on top and decorate with orange zest.

CHOCOLATE-ORANGE SOUP

This luscious soup is a chocolate lover's dream come true. Use good quality Continental chocolate for the best flavor.

SERVES 6

1¼ cups milk
1 vanilla bean
7 ounces bittersweet chocolate
3 egg yolks
2 tablespoons sugar

⅛ cup freshly squeezed, strained orange juice
1 tablespoon Cointreau or Grand Marnier
½ cup whipping cream
chocolate, for decorating

❶ Put the vanilla bean and milk in a medium saucepan and bring just to a boil over medium-high heat, stirring frequently. Remove from the heat and cover. Allow to stand for 15–20 minutes and remove the vanilla bean.

❷ Break the chocolate into small pieces and put in a food processor fitted with a steel blade. Process until finely ground.

❸ In a medium bowl, whisk the egg yolks and sugar for 2–3 minutes until thick and creamy. Whisk in the hot milk and return the mixture to the saucepan. With a wooden spoon, stir over medium-low heat until the custard begins to thicken and will coat the back of the spoon (do not allow it to boil or the custard may curdle).

❹ Immediately pour the custard over the chocolate in the food processor and process for 1 minute, or until the chocolate is melted and the mixture is homogenous. Strain into a cold bowl, stir in the orange juice and Cointreau or Grand Marnier and leave to cool, stirring occasionally. When cool, press clear film against the surface and refrigerate until cold.

❺ Divide the chocolate soup between six chilled shallow bowls, swirl some cream in each and decorate with shaved chocolate curls.

~.~.~.~.~.~.~.~.~.~

COOK'S TIP
To make shaved chocolate curls, hold a bittersweet chocolate bar between your hands for a few seconds to soften it slightly. Using a vegetable peeler, scrape along the length of the edge. Chill the chocolate curls until needed for decorating.

~.~.~.~.~.~.~.~.~.~

LEMON-WINE SOUP

This soup, based on a classic Italian dessert, *zabaglione*, features the fresh tangy flavor of lemon to balance the sweetness of the wine. The mixture triples in volume, so be sure to use a large bowl.

SERVES 4

5 egg yolks
⅓ cup sugar, or more to taste
zest and juice of 1 medium
  lemon (unwaxed or
  scrubbed)
1 cup sweet white wine, such as
  Muscat or Sauternes

2 cups fresh berries
  (raspberries, strawberries or
  blueberries), hulled or
  stemmed if necessary, or 2
  ripe peaches, stoned, peeled
  and sliced

❶ Half-fill a large saucepan with hot water and set over low heat (do not allow the water to boil). Put the egg yolks, sugar, lemon zest and juice in a large heatproof bowl which just fits into the pan without touching the water. Set the bowl over the water and, using an electric mixer at low speed or a balloon whisk, beat the mixture, gradually adding the wine. Continue cooking, beating constantly, until it is thick and fluffy, about 10 minutes.

❷ Remove from the heat and continue beating for about 4 minutes until the mixture is cooler.

❸ Refrigerate, covered, until cold. To serve, stir the soup gently, divide among chilled glass bowls and arrange the fruit on top.

CHAPTER SIX

Cold Soups

Cold soups are refreshing to both the cook and the diner on sweltering days. They are perfect to revive flagging appetites when temperatures soar and make a cooling start to a light summer meal — as soothing as shade in the shimmering heat. To help you keep your cool in the kitchen, many of these soups feature raw ingredients. They all offer vibrant flavors and creative combinations to renew the jaded palate and wilting spirit.

COLD SOUPS

*T*he following sampler of cold soups is drawn from diverse origins, but many are from countries with hot climates. This seems logical, notwithstanding a tradition of steaming hot, spicy soups in these countries, as well.

Cold soups are satisfying in so many ways. The tangy union of tomato and citrus, the icy crunch of cucumber – what could be more refreshing? These soups are designed to cool you down without filling you up.

Flavors tend to fade when chilled, so season more liberally than when preparing hot soups. More forthright flavors are appropriate in soups where garlic or spices predominate, but you

~.~.~.~.~.~.~.~.~.~

"I live on good soup, not on fine words."

Les Femmes savantes
Moliére, 1622–73

~.~.~.~.~.~.~.~.~.~

Cold soups are most often served in warm weather when vegetables are at their peak. Garden fresh vegetables with their full ripe flavor are the best choice for these soups because they won't fade too much when chilled, but generous seasoning is also called for.

will probably also need to use basic seasonings like salt and herbs more generously than usual.

Many soups traditionally served hot are equally delicious cold. Puréed vegetable soups, in particular, offer this versatility — in fact, the selection in this chapter is entirely vegetable-based with meat or seafood for embellishment. Try a spoonful before reheating a soup destined for serving hot to see if you like it cold. Use your imagination and experiment.

Serving cold soups really cold is worth the small effort required. Chill them well. If time is short or the weather is hot, set the container in a bowl of crushed ice prior to ladling the soup out. You can even use this system for individual servings, setting a small bowl inside a larger bowl of finely crushed ice, but at least serve the soup in ice-cold bowls or glasses. Put them in the freezer briefly if there is room. Some of these soups are customarily served with ice cubes floating in them, a good way to keep them cold.

RED PEPPER SOUP
with PRAWNS

The sunny Mediterranean flavors of this cold, refreshing soup will make you think you are sipping it on the Riviera.

SERVES 6

6 large red bell peppers
1 tablespoon vegetable oil
1 pound leeks, thinly sliced
1 large onion, halved and thinly sliced
½ fennel bulb, thinly sliced
¼ teaspoon crushed red pepper flakes
1 cup water

salt and freshly ground pepper
1½ cups garlic stock (see page 16), or more water
fresh lemon juice, to taste
6 tablespoons sour cream or crème fraîche
6 ounces small peeled shrimp, for garnishing

❶ Preheat the oven to 400°F. Put the peppers in a baking dish and roast for about 55 minutes, turning a quarter-turn every 15 minutes, until the peppers are wrinkly and the skin has begun to darken. Put them in a plastic storage box or bag, close tightly and allow to steam for 30 minutes. Halve the peppers and remove the core, seeds and skin. Roughly chop the pepper flesh.

❷ Heat the oil in a large saucepan over medium heat. Add the leeks and onion, and cook, covered, until just softened, about 5 minutes. Stir in the fennel, pepper flakes and roasted peppers. Add the water and a little salt and pepper, and simmer over medium-low heat for about 30 minutes, until all the vegetables are tender.

❸ Transfer the vegetables and cooking liquid to a blender or a food processor fitted with a steel blade and purée until smooth.

❹ In a bowl, combine the purée and stock or additional water, leave to cool, then cover and refrigerate until cold. When ready to serve, taste and adjust the seasoning and add a few drops of lemon juice. Ladle the soup into chilled bowls or soup plates, put a dollop of sour cream or *crème fraîche* on each and arrange the shrimp on the cream, dividing them evenly.

~.~.~.~.~.~.~.~.~

TO DRINK
A rosé from
Provence or well-
chilled Pineau des
Charentes.

~.~.~.~.~.~.~.~.~

CORDOBAN GAZPACHO

(*Salmorejo*)

This cold soup from Cordoba is refreshing on a hot day. The recipe is adapted from the soup served at El Caballo Rojo, a fine restaurant in the old part of the city, and is one of many versions of gazpacho found in Andalucía. A blender gives a smooth texture and saves time on preparation. If it is necessary to use a food processor, it is best to peel and seed the tomatoes first and strain the soup after puréeing.

SERVES 6-8

10 ounces stale French bread
2 pounds ripe tomatoes, washed and cored
1 small onion, quartered
2 garlic cloves, crushed
2 teaspoons sherry vinegar
6 tablespoons extra-virgin olive oil

salt

TO GARNISH
2 hard-boiled eggs, sliced
3 ounces sliced Spanish ham, cut in matchstick slivers

❶ Trim the crusts from the bread, cut into thick slices and cover with cold water. Remove the bread, squeeze out the water and put the bread in a blender.

❷ Cut the tomatoes into quarters and add them to the soaked bread with the onion, garlic and vinegar.

❸ Blend the ingredients for several minutes until completely puréed, scraping the sides of the blender as necessary.

❹ Slowly add the olive oil through the hole in the top. If you wish, thin the soup with a little ice water (the soup should be thick). Season to taste with salt.

❺ Refrigerate the soup until cold. Ladle into chilled bowls and garnish with slices of egg and slivers of ham.

~.~.~.~.~.~.~.~.~

COOK'S TIP
To peel tomatoes, remove the
core and cut a shallow cross in the
base, cover with boiling water for
10 seconds, drain, then immerse in cold
water and drain again. Cut in half
and scrape out the seeds into a strainer
to extract the juice. Add the
juice to the soup.

~.~.~.~.~.~.~.~.~

CHILLED GREEN PEA SOUP

This soup is a stunning bright green color. It is simple to make and quite tasty using frozen peas, but if you are able to find fresh-picked young garden peas, you are in for a real gourmet treat.

SERVES 6

1 tablespoon butter	*⅔ cup whipping cream*
4 shallots, finely chopped	*2 tablespoons chopped fresh*
6 cups shelled fresh peas or	*mint*
thawed frozen peas	*12–18 small snow peas,*
4 cups water	*blanched and chilled, for*
salt and freshly ground pepper	*garnishing*

❶ Melt the butter in a large saucepan over medium-low heat. Add the shallots and cook, stirring occasionally, until they begin to soften, about 5 minutes.
❷ Add the peas and water. Season with salt and a little pepper. Simmer covered, stirring occasionally, until the vegetables are tender, about 12 minutes for frozen or young fresh peas, or up to 18 minutes for large or older peas.
❸ Transfer the solids to a blender or a food processor fitted with a steel blade. Add some of the cooking liquid and purée until smooth, working in batches if necessary. Strain into a bowl with the remaining cooking liquid, allow to stand until cool, cover and refrigerate until cold.
❹ Using an electric mixer or whisk, whip the cream in a chilled bowl until soft peaks form. Stir in the mint.
❺ Thin the soup with a little cold water, if needed, and adjust the seasoning. Ladle into chilled soup plates and garnish each with a dollop of cream and 2 or 3 snow peas.

COOK'S TIP
You will need
5 to 6 pounds of fresh
peas in the pod to
obtain 6 cups of
shelled peas.

CUCUMBER COOLER

This soup is so refreshing – cool as the proverbial cucumber with a subtle hint of mint.

SERVES 6

2 large cucumbers	*2 tablespoons finely chopped*
1¼ cups plain yogurt	*fresh mint*
(preferably Greek-style)	*salt and freshly ground pepper*
¾ cup buttermilk	*fresh lemon juice*
1–2 garlic cloves, very finely	*mint leaves, for garnishing*
minced	

❶ Cut 12 thin slices from one of the cucumbers and reserve, covered, for garnishing. Peel the cucumbers, halve lengthwise and scoop out the seeds with the tip of a small sharp spoon.
❷ Grate the cucumbers and transfer to a large bowl. Stir in the yogurt, buttermilk, garlic and mint. Season to taste with salt and pepper and a few drops of lemon juice.
❸ Refrigerate until cold, at least 1 hour. Ladle into chilled soup plates and garnish with the reserved cucumber slices and mint leaves.

COLD BORSCHT

There is no single definitive recipe for Borscht, the popular Eastern European peasant soup. In fact, there seem to be to almost limitless variations – some with meat, some with beans, some mainly cabbage, others mainly beets. This meatless version offers a balanced combination of vegetable flavors that meld when chilled.

SERVES 6

½ medium red cabbage, cored and coarsely chopped
1 tablespoon vegetable oil
1 large onion, chopped
1 large leek, split and sliced
1 large carrot, thinly sliced
1 medium parsnip, thinly sliced
⅔ cup red wine
5 cups chicken stock or water, plus more if needed

6 medium beets, peeled and cubed
4 tomatoes, peeled, seeded and coarsely chopped
bay leaf
1 teaspoon sherry vinegar or red wine vinegar
sour cream or yogurt
chopped fresh dill, for garnishing

❶ Cover the cabbage with cold water. Set over high heat, bring to the boil and boil for 3 minutes. Drain.
❷ Heat the oil in a large saucepan over medium-low heat and add the onion and leek. Cover and sweat the vegetables until soft, about 5 minutes, stirring occasionally. Add the carrot, parsnip, blanched cabbage and wine. Bring to a boil and add the stock or water, beets, tomatoes and bay leaf. Bring back to a boil, reduce the heat and simmer until all the vegetables are tender, about 1¼ hours.
❸ Remove the bay leaf and, using a slotted spoon, transfer the solids to a blender or a food processor fitted with a steel blade, working in batches if necessary. Add some of the cooking liquid and purée until smooth. Strain the purée and any remaining cooking liquid into a large bowl. Stir in the vinegar, leave to cool and refrigerate until cold.
❹ If you wish, thin the soup with water or more stock. Season to taste with salt and pepper, and add a little more vinegar, if liked. Ladle into chilled soup bowls or plates, top each with a dollop of sour cream or yogurt and sprinkle lightly with dill.

~·~·~·~·~·~·~·~·~

To Drink
Sparkling
red wine.

~·~·~·~·~·~·~·~·~

LAVENDER VICHYSSOISE

Use blue potatoes with deeply colored flesh for this soup. If made from pale blue potatoes the soup will be grey, not pale purple. The flavor of lavender is pervasive, so a tiny amount is sufficient.

SERVES 6–8

1 tablespoon butter
1 large shallot (mauve if possible), finely chopped
1 pound blue potatoes, cubed
5 cups chicken stock
3 large leeks, white part only, split and thinly sliced

pinch of lavender flowers
salt and white pepper
⅔ cup whipping cream
3 tablespoons chopped fresh chives, for garnishing
chive flowers, for garnishing

❶ Melt the butter in a large saucepan over medium heat. Add the shallot and cook until just softened, about 5 minutes. Add the potatoes and stock, and bring to a boil over high heat. Reduce the heat to medium-low and simmer for about 25 minutes, stirring occasionally.
❷ When the potatoes are just tender when pierced, stir in the leeks. Add the lavender and a little salt and pepper. Simmer for 10–15 minutes longer until the vegetables are soft and tender, stirring occasionally.
❸ Transfer the solids to a blender or a food processor fitted with a steel blade. Add some of the cooking liquid and purée until smooth, working in batches if necessary.
❹ Strain the mixture into a bowl, pressing firmly with the back of a spoon to extract as much liquid as possible. Stir in the cream and, if the soup seems too thick, thin it with a little more stock or water. Allow to cool and refrigerate until cold. Ladle into chilled bowls or cups and garnish with chives and chive flowers.

~·~·~·~·~·~·~·~·~

COOK'S TIP
If blue (purple-fleshed) potatoes are difficult to find, use white potatoes and peel them before cooking.

~·~·~·~·~·~·~·~·~

ICED ALMOND *and* GARLIC SOUP

This recipe dates from the tenth century when the Moors inhabited Andalucía. It is one of numerous versions of gazpacho popular all over Spain. This version is typical of Málaga, where almond trees flourish.

SERVES 4

3 cups soft white bread crumbs, made from flavorful homemade-style bread
1½ cups blanched almonds, lightly toasted
2 garlic cloves, minced

pinch of salt
2 teaspoons sherry vinegar
6 tablespoons extra-virgin olive oil
3 cups water
1 cup seedless white grapes, for garnishing

❶ Soak the breadcrumbs in cold water to cover for 5 minutes.
❷ Put the almonds, garlic and salt in a food processor fitted with a steel blade and process until the nuts are finely ground. Strain the breadcrumbs, pressing with the back of a spoon to extract more water. Add to the almond mixture and process until pasty.
❸ Add the vinegar and, with the machine running, pour the oil through the feed tube, then slowly pour in the water, stopping to scrape down the sides several times. Strain into a bowl and refrigerate until very cold.
❹ Ladle over ice cubes into a chilled tureen or soup plates and garnish with the grapes.

ICED TOMATO *and* ORANGE SOUP

This lean, flavorful soup depends on ripe tomatoes. Use seasonal sun-ripened tomatoes at their peak – plum tomatoes are best.

SERVES 4

2 teaspoons olive oil
1 large sweet onion, chopped
1 medium carrot, chopped
2 ½ pounds ripe tomatoes, cored and quartered
1 orange (unwaxed or scrubbed), thinly sliced
bouquet garni (thyme and

marjoram sprigs and bay leaf)
1 cup water
salt and freshly ground pepper
½ cup fresh orange juice
mint sprigs, for garnishing

❶ Heat the olive oil in a large nonreactive saucepan or flameproof casserole over medium heat. Add the onion and carrot, and cook for 4–5 minutes, stirring occasionally, until the onion is just softened.

❷ Add the tomatoes, orange and *bouquet garni*. Reduce the heat to medium-low, cover and simmer for about 40 minutes, stirring once or twice, until the vegetables are very soft.

❸ Work the tomato mixture through a food mill fitted with a fine blade set over a bowl. Add the orange juice and season to taste with salt and pepper. Strain the soup, allow to cool, cover and refrigerate until cold. Serve in glasses, with ice cubes if you like, and garnish with mint sprigs.

COLD AVOCADO SOUP

This spicy soup is like a guacamole that you can drink. The best avocados to use are the very large ones with bright green skin, such as Lula or Ettinger varieties. Haas avocados, smaller with dark pebbly skin, will do, but they discolor quickly and can darken the soup.

SERVES 4–6

4 cups chicken stock
6 garlic cloves, chopped
bouquet garni (parsley stems, thyme and marjoram sprigs)
2 large avocados, about 1 pound each, ripe but not soft
3–4 tablespoons fresh lime juice
2–3 teaspoons chopped jalapeño peppers

1 cup sour cream
salt
Tabasco sauce
2 plum tomatoes, peeled, seeded and finely chopped
3 scallions, finely chopped
2–3 tablespoons chopped fresh cilantro

❶ Combine the stock and garlic in a saucepan and bring to the boil over high heat, skimming off any foam that rises to the surface. Add the *bouquet garni*, reduce the heat to low and simmer for 30 minutes, or until the stock tastes of garlic. Strain into a bowl, allow to cool and refrigerate until cold. Remove any congealed fat.

❷ Shortly before serving, cut the avocados in half, discard the stones and scoop the flesh into a blender or a food processor fitted with a steel blade. Add the lime juice and jalapeños. Remove any congealed fat from the stock, add half of it and purée until smooth, scraping down the sides as necessary. Add as much of the remaining stock as the capacity of the blender or processor permits and process to combine.

❸ Transfer the mixture to a large bowl. Stir in any remaining stock and a third of the soured cream. Season with salt and Tabasco to taste, adding more lime juice if you like. Ladle into chilled small bowls or glass punch cups. Dollop on the remaining sour cream and sprinkle each serving with chopped tomatoes, scallions and cilantro, dividing them evenly.

~.~.~.~.~.~.~.~.~

TO DRINK
Margaritas or ice-cold
Aquavit.

~.~.~.~.~.~.~.~.~

CHAPTER SEVEN

Clear Soups

SHIMMERING LUCID LIQUID LIFTS THE
SPIRIT AND TEASES THE APPETITE. LIGHT
AND BRIMMING WITH WELL BALANCED FLAVORS —
RICH STOCK, AROMATIC VEGETABLES AND HERBS —
PERFECT CONSOMMÉS ARE CONSIDERED A TRUE
TEST OF CULINARY SKILL. MADE IN THE
TRADITIONAL WAY, THEY CAN BE DEMANDING, BUT
MANY OF THE CLEAR SOUPS THAT FOLLOW ARE
SIMPLER CREATIONS, A UNION OF CLASSIC CUISINE
AND THE REQUIREMENTS OF MODERN LIVING.

CLEAR SOUPS

*P*urists would argue that only consommés can be classed as
clear soups. Those are here, and they are worth making.
But I take a broader view and so here, too, are soups which are
essentially light broths, enveloping and providing the backdrop for
other ingredients in them.

    *The liquid element is the most important, and all these soups
must be made with flavorful homemade stock. Seize the moment
when you have good rich stock available.*

    *The additional ingredients are really embellishments for the
stock. In classic French cuisine, these are called garnishes, and they
offer the opportunity for endless variety. Consommés, in particular,
have a traditional repertoire of embellishments, such as a
sprinkling of herbs, finely diced or slivered vegetables or pieces of*

*"I believe I was once
considerably scandalized
by her declaring that clear
soup was a more
important factor in life
than a clear conscience."*

SAKI (H. H. MUNRO)
1870–1916

~·~·~·~·~·~·~·~·~·~

Light and limpid clear soups need
simple, colorful garnishes such as
fresh herbs or bright slivers of vegetables
to bring an added dimension of flavor
and highlight their clarity.

*egg custard cut into pretty shapes, each giving the soup a different
name. A clear, shimmering, flavorful consommé is considered a test
of culinary skill and a worthy accomplishment.*

*In principle, all of these soups could utilize clarified stock, but
if the stock is relatively limpid – clear enough to see what is in the
soup – clarification is only necessary for consommés. Even then,
if you "brew" the stock slowly, it may be acceptably clear.*

*Serve these soups in a way that accentuates their clarity and
allows any ingredients in them to be seen. Glass bowls or white
porcelain are ideal.*

*A clear soup makes a perfect starter – light and not too filling to
prevent the enjoyment of what is to follow. Servings are generally
small and the yield calculated in the recipes reflects this. Naturally
these soups can be made more substantial by adding more
embellishments and serving in larger portions, if you wish.*

BEEF CONSOMME *with* PARMESAN PUFFS

Consommé is a classic starter before a rich, elaborate meal, as it stimulates the palate and whets the appetite without filling. The method for clarifying stock is the same for any kind, but the ingredients to flavor the consommé are chosen to suit each one. Garnishes also vary; they should be a light adjunct offering a bit of contrast and novelty.

SERVES 6

8 cups strong fat-free beef stock	*1 tomato, finely chopped*
¾–1 pound very lean ground beef	*1 small bunch fresh parsley, finely chopped*
2 leeks, finely chopped	*2 teaspoons dried tarragon*
1 onion, finely chopped	*2 egg whites*
1 carrot, finely chopped	*Parmesan puffs (see page 123), for garnishing*

❶ Put the ground beef in a large saucepan with the leeks, onion, carrot, tomato, parsley and dried tarragon. Add the egg whites, mix to combine and stir in the stock. Set over high heat and stir almost continuously as the mixture comes to a boil. When it begins to tremble, reduce the heat to low and simmer very gently, without stirring or disturbing it, for 30 minutes. Carefully lift off about half of the solid covering, using a slotted spoon, and ladle the clarified stock through a sieve lined with damp muslin into a saucepan. (Discard the solid matter.) Blot any grease from the surface with paper towels.

❷ Bring the consommé just to simmering, ladle into warm soup plates or bowls and garnish with Parmesan puffs, or use other garnishes if you prefer, such as those described below.

GARNISHES FOR CONSOMMES

chopped fresh herbs	*thinly sliced mushrooms*
finely diced root vegetables, parboiled and drained	*diced or sliced truffle*
julienne strips of carrot, celery, leeks or spring onions, parboiled and drained	*thin eggy crêpes made with chopped herbs, sliced into strips*
finely diced, peeled and seeded tomato	*thin ribbons of spinach or leaf lettuce*
thinly sliced or diced bell peppers (roasted, peeled and seeded)	*strips of cooked beef, chicken, ham or other meat*
	cooked rice, barley or noodles
	cooked filled pasta

GAME BIRD CONSOMME *with* POACHED QUAIL EGGS

This is not a classic consommé, as it is not clarified. Cooking it slowly is an easy and effective method to achieve a relatively clear stock and retain the delicate flavor that would be lost in the clarification process.

SERVES 4

1 large game bird carcass, such as pheasant or duck, or 3–4 small ones, such as pigeon or quail, raw or cooked and trimmed of excess fat	*1 tablespoon black peppercorns*
	bouquet garni (thyme sprigs, parsley stems, tarragon or sage leaves and bay leaf)
1 large onion, quartered	*3 cups cold chicken stock*
2 carrots, coarsely chopped	*salt (optional)*
1 parsnip, coarsely chopped	*2–3 tablespoons dry sherry*
1 leek, sliced	*8 quail eggs*
2–4 garlic cloves, crushed	*fresh chervil or flat-leaf parsley, for garnishing*

❶ Put the carcass(es), onion, carrots, parsnip, leek, garlic, peppercorns and *bouquet garni* in a stockpot or large heavy saucepan. Add the stock and enough cold water to cover the ingredients by 1 inch. Bring slowly to a boil over medium heat, skimming the foam that rises to the surface often. Reduce the heat to low and simmer for 1½–2 hours. Strain the stock through a strainer lined with damp cheesecloth into a bowl and if any meat can be picked off the carcass, reserve it. Cool the stock and refrigerate for several hours or overnight. Skim off any congealed fat and blot the surface with a paper towel to remove any remaining fat.

❷ Bring a small pan of salted water to a boil and poach the quail eggs, a few at a time, for 2–3 minutes, or until done as you like them. Remove with a slotted spoon to a bowl of tepid water to stop further cooking. Trim off any untidy bits of white.

❸ Bring the stock just to a boil and reduce the heat to medium-low. Taste and season with a little salt, if needed, and stir in the sherry. If the stock is bland, reduce it slightly with a fresh *bouquet garni*.

❹ Place the eggs in warm shallow soup plates, ladle over the consommé and garnish with chervil or parsley leaves.

WONTON SOUP

This light and delicious soup has universal appeal. The small dumplings are a popular snack in China and are sometimes served crisply fried.

SERVES 6

½ ounce dried Oriental	*pinch of Oriental 5-spice*
mushrooms	*powder (optional)*
8 ounces lean boneless	*1tsp soy sauce*
pork, cubed	*1 egg, separated*
⅔ cup fresh spinach leaves	*24 wonton wrappers*
2–3 scallions, coarsely chopped	*8 cups chicken stock*
1 garlic clove, minced	*finely slivered scallions,*
	for garnishing

❶ Put the dried mushrooms in a small bowl and cover with boiling water. Allow to soak for about 20 minutes. Drain and blot dry. Chop finely.

❷ Combine the pork, spinach leaves, scallions and garlic in a food processor fitted with a steel blade and pulse until finely chopped, or chop finely with a large knife. Add the 5-spice powder, if using, the soy sauce and egg yolk, and pulse, or stir, until mixed. Beat the egg white with 1 teaspoon of water in a small bowl.

❸ Place 6 wonton wrappers on a work surface. Put a rounded teaspoonful of filling in the center of each wrapper. Brush egg white around the filling. Bring the edges together to enclose the filling and twist, pressing together to secure. Continue filling the remaining wonton wrappers.

❹ Bring a large quantity of salted water to a boil. Drop in half the wontons, bring back to a boil and cook for 3–4 minutes until they have come to the surface and the wonton dough is tender. Drain on a clean kitchen towel and cook the remainder.

❺ Meanwhile, bring the stock to a boil in a large saucepan. Divide the wontons between 6 warm bowls, sprinkle with scallions and ladle the hot stock over them.

ROASTED GARLIC SOUP

This soup has a mellow, almost smoky, garlic flavor that makes it immensely satisfying yet very light. A strong well-flavored stock is essential and it should be relatively clear, to see the croutons. It is inspired by the Mediterranean peasant soups found in France, Italy, Spain and Portugal.

SERVES 4

1 large head large-clove garlic, about 3½ ounces
4 cups chicken or beef stock
2–3 slices white bread, crusts trimmed
finely chopped fresh parsley, for garnishing

❶ Preheat the oven to 400°F. Wrap the garlic, whole, in foil and bake for about 40 minutes until very soft.

❷ Bring the stock just to a boil over medium heat. Remove and set aside 3 cloves of the garlic, put the rest of the head into the stock and press with a wooden spoon to crush it lightly. Reduce the heat to low and simmer gently, partially covered, for 30 minutes, or until the stock has taken on the flavor of the garlic.

❸ Cut the bread into 12 squares or diamond shapes about 1¼ inches on each side. Place on a baking sheet and toast the bread lightly. Squeeze out the garlic from the reserved garlic cloves and spread on the croûtons.

❹ Place the croûtons in the bottom of warm soup plates. Strain the soup to remove the garlic and ladle it over the croûtons, dividing evenly among the soup plates. Sprinkle with parsley and serve.

TORTILLA SOUP

The crunchy tortilla strips bring a satisfying element of contrast to this light soup. If you prefer, pass them separately, along with chopped scallions and cilantro. In Mexico, small cubes of cheese are sometimes added.

SERVES 6

2 teaspoons vegetable oil, plus more for frying
1 small onion, finely chopped
3 garlic cloves, minced
8 cups chicken stock
¼ teaspoon crushed red pepper flakes
¼ teaspoon each dried thyme and oregano
fresh parsley and cilantro stems
bay leaf
salt
6–8 corn tortillas
5 tomatoes (preferably plum), peeled, seeded and diced
1 avocado, stoned, peeled and diced

TO GARNISH
3–4 scallions, finely chopped
2–3 tablespoons chopped fresh cilantro

❶ Heat the oil in a large saucepan over medium heat. Add the onion and garlic, and cook until softened, 3–4 minutes. Stir in the stock and add the red pepper flakes, herbs and a little salt. Simmer, partially covered, for about 30 minutes, stirring occasionally.

❷ Stack the tortillas and cut into strips ½ inch wide and 2 inches long. In a medium-sized frying pan, add oil to a depth of about ½ inch. Set over medium-high heat and when the oil begins to smoke, fry the tortilla strips in batches until crisp and lightly browned, about 1 minute. Remove with a slotted spoon and drain on paper towels. Keep warm in a slow oven.

❸ Strain the soup into a clean saucepan, stir in the tomatoes and simmer gently over low heat for 5 minutes, or until heated through. Add the avocado, cook for 1–2 minutes longer and ladle the soup into warm bowls. Garnish with tortilla strips, scallions and cilantro.

SEAFOOD RAVIOLI *in* BOUILLON

These filled pasta pillows are easy to make and lend themselves to all sorts of fillings. Vary the seafood in the filling according to what is available, using cooked fish, clams or scallops, chopped, to make about 8 ounces seafood.

SERVES 8

6 cups seafood stock
fresh cilantro leaves, to garnish
PASTA
1 cup flour, plus more for
    dusting
¼ teaspoon salt
1 whole egg
1 egg, separated
1 teaspoon olive oil
2–3 tablespoons cold water

FILLING
¼ cup crabmeat
¼ cup small peeled cooked
    shrimp, chopped
2 teaspoons finely chopped
    parsley
2 teaspoons finely chopped fresh
    cilantro
1 teaspoon finely chopped
    chives
freshly ground black pepper
lemon juice
1½ tablespoons whipping cream

❶ For the pasta, put the flour and salt into a food processor fitted with a steel blade and pulse to combine. In a small bowl, beat together the egg, egg yolk, oil and 2 tablespoons of the water. With the machine running, pour in the mixture and process until it forms a ball which leaves the bowl virtually clean. If the dough seems crumbly, add the remaining water; if it seems sticky, add 1–2 tablespoons flour and continue kneading until it forms a ball. Wrap and chill for at least 30 minutes. Set aside the egg white in a small dish.
❷ For the filling, drain the crabmeat and shrimp well. Combine with the herbs in a bowl. Season with pepper and a few drops of lemon juice, and stir in the cream until well mixed.
❸ Divide the pasta dough into quarters and keep the remaining dough wrapped while you roll out one quarter. Using a pasta machine and starting on the thickest setting, roll through the dough, each time on successively thinner settings. (The dough should be thin enough to begin to see through but not tear easily.) Lay the strip of dough on a lightly floured work surface and cut in half. Place 4 rounded teaspoonfuls of filling at even intervals along one half. Brush around the filling with egg white and lay the remaining half of the strip over the top. Press gently but firmly to seal. Cut out with a 3-inch round cutter or cut into squares. Arrange

the ravioli in one layer on a baking sheet dusted generously with flour and repeat with the remaining dough. Leave the ravioli to dry in a cool place for about 15 minutes or refrigerate for 1–2 hours.
❹ Bring a large quantity of salted water to a boil and cook the ravioli, a few at a time, until the pasta is just tender, about 3 minutes. Drain on a clean tea towel while cooking the remainder.
❺ Meanwhile, bring the stock to a boil in a large saucepan. Divide the ravioli between warm shallow soup plates, ladle over the stock and float a few cilantro leaves on each.

LEMON EGG DROP SOUP

(Avegolemono)

This traditional Greek soup has its counterparts in Italy and China. It is essentially simple, but depends on a rich flavorful stock. Fish stock may be used instead of chicken, and rice is often added.

SERVES 4

4 cups chicken stock
2 eggs
3 tablespoons fresh lemon juice,
    or to taste

salt and freshly ground pepper
2 tablespoons chopped fresh
    parsley

❶ Bring the stock to a boil in a large saucepan over medium-high heat. Reduce the heat to medium-low so it just simmers.
❷ In a small bowl or measuring cup, beat the eggs and lemon juice with a fork until combined. Season with salt and pepper.
❸ Beat a few tablespoons of the stock into the egg mixture, then very slowly pour the mixture into the soup, whisking slowly and constantly with the fork until the egg is set.
❹ Taste and adjust the seasoning, adding more lemon juice if you wish. Ladle the soup into warm bowls and sprinkle with parsley.

Tarragon Chicken Consomme
with Chicken Quenelles

A richly flavored, sparkling clear consommé is considered a true indicator of culinary skill. Although it is relatively expensive and time-consuming, it is worth making the effort at least once. Start with strong homemade stock, as the clarification process steals some of the flavor, in spite of the additional flavoring ingredients. Reduce your stock, if necessary, to concentrate the flavor before beginning.

SERVES 6

1 skinless boneless chicken breast, about 7 ounces
2 small leeks, finely chopped
1 onion, finely chopped
1 celery stalk, finely chopped
3–4 sprigs fresh parsley, finely chopped
2 teaspoons dried tarragon
2 egg whites
8 cups strong fat-free chicken stock
chopped fresh tarragon leaves, for garnishing

Chicken Quenelles
1 skinless boneless chicken breast, well chilled, about 7 ounces
1 egg white
1 tablespoon chopped fresh tarragon
4 tablespoons whipping cream, well chilled
salt and freshly ground pepper
freshly grated nutmeg

❶ Finely chop the chicken breast in a food processor or by hand. Put in a large saucepan with the leeks, onion, celery, parsley and dried tarragon. Add the egg whites, mix to combine and stir in the stock. Set over high heat and stir almost continuously as the mixture comes to a boil. When it begins to tremble, reduce the heat to low and simmer very gently, without stirring or disturbing it, for 30 minutes. Carefully lift off about a third of the solid covering, using a slotted spoon, and ladle the clarified stock through a strainer lined with damp cheesecloth. (Discard the solid matter.)

❷ For the chicken quenelles, cut the chicken breast into large pieces, put in a food processor fitted with a steel blade and process until smooth. Add the egg white and tarragon, and mix until combined. Add the cream by spoonfuls. Do not overprocess or the mixture will become warm and the cream will not be readily absorbed. Season generously and refrigerate for at least 15 minutes.

❸ Bring a pan of salted water to a simmer. Using two teaspoons, shape the chicken mixture into small ovals and drop into the water a few at a time. Poach for about 2 minutes until they float and feel firm to the touch. Drain on clean kitchen towels.

❹ Bring the consommé just to a boil over medium-high heat. Divide the quenelles between warmed shallow soup plates, ladle over the consommé and sprinkle with a little chopped tarragon.

CHAPTER EIGHT

Garnishes and Accompaniments

MOST SOUPS BENEFIT FROM EMBELLISH-
MENT AND IT IS THE PERFECT ARENA
TO GIVE YOUR IMAGINATION FREE REIN. THE
OPTIONS FOR GARNISHES AND ACCOMPANIMENTS
ARE SO BROAD AND FLEXIBLE THAT ALMOST ANY-
THING GOES. THEY CAN BE AS SIMPLE AS A FEW
FRESH HERBS, AS ARTISTIC AS A FEATHERY DESIGN
IN CREAM, AS SATISFYING AS A RAFT OF BREAD
WITH BUBBLING CHEESE – AND THEY ALWAYS
BRING A BIT OF FLAIR AND EXCITEMENT.

GARNISHES *and* ACCOMPANIMENTS

*S*ome sort of embellishment gives even the simplest soup a real lift and adds interest. Garnishes and accompaniments are especially important to complete and enhance the experience when soup is served as the main course.

Soups embellishments can be anything from sauces to stir in, like Provençal basil purée with olive oil, to pasta parcels or herb dumplings, to a simple swirl of cream on top. The idea is to provide visual interest and a flavor lift.

Bread in one form or another is the most common soup garnish. In fact, the earliest soup was hot liquid poured over bread and ever since, it has played an integral role in the consumption of soup. Croutons made from bread come in all shapes and sizes, bread crumbs may be the binding for dumplings and bread itself is sometimes used as a thickener in puréed soups. A simple loaf of crusty bread is often the most satisfying partner to soup.

Other Embellishments

Some soups have traditional garnishes without which they seem incomplete. Fish soups in France are often served with garlicky mayonnaise-like sauces – *rouille* and *aïoli* – in addition to croutons. These can give a lift to other kinds of soup as well, such as Chicken Minestroni. These powerful sauces are best in robust soups, as is the basil purée from the Provençal Vegetable Soup.

Consommés and clear soups need embellishment and they offer a perfect opportunity to experiment with all sorts of garnishes. You can vary a soup significantly by changing its accompaniment. For example, you could put chicken quenelles in Tarragon Chicken Consommé, as in the recipe, or alternatively, add herb dumplings, homemade noodles, poached quail eggs (all in this book) or other things you are likely to have handy, such as cooked rice, finely diced tomatoes or thin ribbons of spinach.

Serving with Flair

It is difficult to give precise guidelines for anything as individual as creativity and style. The less confined you feel by rules, the better. Give your imagination free rein. Experiment and don't worry if it doesn't work out perfectly.

Create drama with color contrast. This can be the whiteness of sour cream on deep red borscht, a brilliant orange roasted pepper purée on pale brown eggplant soup or yellow nasturtium blossoms on asparagus soup. The Victorians had a penchant for creating a whole meal of food of the same color, but dramatic impact is easier to achieve with contrast.

The attraction of most garnishes is the visual element, but a contrast of texture is also appealing. Crispy fried onions or crumbled bacon sprinkled over a creamy soup brings a delightful element of surprise.

Use something in an unexpected way, such as sprinkling thin ribbons of fresh spinach instead of chopped parsley when an herbal garnish is appropriate, or using whole sprigs of basil leaves instead of chopped ones. Something as simple as freezing mint leaves, or other herbs or small pieces of fruit or vegetables, into ice cubes destined to chill cold savory soups or fruit soups makes a dramatic impression. What you freeze in these ice cubes should, of course, be clean and identifiable.

Select flavors that work together. For example, chive flowers would be better on Sweet Potato and Leek Soup than on Sesame Carrot and Parsnip because the chive flavor echoes the leek, both being of the onion family.

Edible flowers make simple yet appealing garnishes, as long as they have not been sprayed. Many supermarkets now carry edible flowers, so that is a good source. Avoid flowers from florists and nurseries, as these have usually been exposed to pesticides. The flowers of common culinary herbs are edible, so if you have a garden – or a friend who has – use basil, borage, chive, mint, rosemary and thyme flowers, among others. Equally, some fruit and vegetable blooms make colorful garnishes; try using the flowers of beans, various squashes or cherries, again from a source you know. Not all flowers are safe to eat or use with food, so consult a specialist if you want to be sure. Otherwise stay with rose petals, primroses, pansies, violets, lavender, jasmine, geraniums, nasturtiums, hollyhocks and honeysuckle blossoms, preferably fresh from the garden and unsprayed.

~.~

DECORATIVE ICE BOWL

Flowers, fruit and leaves glowing through ice formed into a bowl make a stunning presentation for a cold soup. You could use all herbs and herb flowers for a savoury cold soup or carry out the theme of a dessert soup by freezing the same fruit in ice. Make sure the ice bowl is large enough to hold what you plan to serve from it. You can make individual bowls if you have enough freezer space for them.

Crushed Ice
2 freezer-safe bowls (preferably tempered glass),
*   at least 8 cup and 10 cup capacities*
ice cubes or ceramic baking beans
a selection of two or three kinds of small edible
*   flowers and other herb flowers and*
*   leaves, free of pesticides*
a selection of two or three
*   kinds of small fruit, such*
*   as blueberries,*
*   red currants,*
*   raspberries, small*
*   strawberries, cherries,*
*   grapes and halved kumquats*

Put a layer of crushed ice in the bottom of the larger bowl. Set the smaller bowl inside and weight it down with ice cubes. Drop some flowers and/or flower petals, some leaves and some fruit into the space between the two bowls. Add some crushed ice to take up some space between the decorative elements and prevent them from floating. Continue filling the space between the bowls with flowers, fruit, leaves and crushed ice. Pour in cold water to come up to the rim of the larger bowl and freeze until firm.

To unmold, pour warm water into the smaller bowl and lift it out as soon as the ice around it starts to melt. Dip the larger bowl in warm water and turn the ice bowl out. If not using immediately, store it in the freezer.

For serving, set the ice bowl on a napkin on a tray or platter and decorate the base, if wished, with more leaves, flowers and fruit.

Baked and Fried Garnishes

CROUTONS

Croutons come in all shapes and sizes, depending on what they are served with, but their crunchy texture always adds interest. Most often, they are simply thin slices of baguette toasted until dry and crisp; these are almost invariably served with French fish soups. Croutons cut from larger diameter loaves, such as those used in classic French Onion Soup to support the cheese that is *gratinéed* on top, are sometimes called *croûtes*. They can also be made from brown bread, cornbread, brioche or other foods used like bread, such as polenta. Most croutons keep well and are easily made in advance, especially when you have stale French bread on hand.

MAKES ABOUT 30, SERVING 6–8
12-inch piece of French bread
(baguette), about 2 inches in
diameter

❶ Preheat the oven to 350°F. Cut the bread into slices about ⅜ inch thick.
❷ Place the slices in one layer on a baking sheet and toast for 8–10 minutes, turning once, or until golden.
❸ Serve hot or allow to cool completely and store in an airtight container for up to 3 days or freeze, well wrapped. Serve at room temperature or warm before serving.

Variations

If you wish, brush the croutons with olive oil after you turn them over. For garlic croutons, rub the toasts with a halved garlic clove after toasting. For a less intense garlic flavor, brush one side with garlic-infused oil after turning over. (To infuse the oil, combine finely chopped garlic with olive oil and set over low heat for about 10 minutes, or until aromatic.)

CUBED CROUTONS To make cubed croutons, cut crustless slices of firm sandwich bread or rustic country bread into ½-inch cubes. Place in a single layer on a baking sheet and toast in a preheated 325°F oven for about 20 minutes until golden, shaking the pan occasionally.
FRIED CROUTONS Both sliced and cubed croutons may be fried instead of toasted. Heat oil to a depth of about

½ inch in a small frying pan over medium-high heat. When it starts to smoke, add the croutons and fry until golden, stirring cubes or turning slices for even browning. Drain on paper towels and serve warm or at room temperature. (Best made within a few hours of serving; warm in a slow oven if made more than 15 minutes in advance.)

Other Croutons

POLENTA CROUTONS Use polenta, molded in a loaf pan until firm, then sliced thinly and cut in squares or diamonds. Cook as for Fried Croutons.
SESAME CROUTONS See Sesame Carrot and Parsnip Soup, page 38.
GOAT'S CHEESE CROUTONS See Roasted Tomato Soup with Goat's Cheese Croutons, page 38.
CROSTINI Crostini are essentially croutons with something on them. In Italy, the topping is often olive spread, anchovy paste, minced cooked chicken livers or cheese. A handy cheese spread for crostini is grated cheese, a little chopped onion and enough mayonnaise to hold it together spread on croutons and grilled.
CORNMEAL FRITTERS See Caramelized Onion Soup with Cornmeal Fritters, page 31.

CHEESE STRAWS

These rich flaky pastries, although a bit fiddly, are worth the effort. They are perfect to accompany creamy vegetable soups, such as Emerald Soup or Cream of Asparagus Soup, as they provide a contrast of texture and taste. They are equally good served with drinks.

MAKES ABOUT 50

1¾ sticks (7 ounces) cold unsalted butter
1½ cups flour
⅔ cup cold water
½ cup freshly grated Gruyère or Parmesan cheese, or a combination
1 egg, beaten with 1 teaspoon water
3–4 tablespoons freshly grated Parmesan cheese

❶ Cut the butter in 14 pieces and put into the freezer for 30 minutes, or until very firm.
❷ Put the flour into a food processor and pulse to combine. Add the butter and pulse three or four times; there should still be big chunks of butter. Run the machine for 5 seconds while pouring the water through the feed tube, then switch off the machine. Turn out the mixture onto a lightly floured cool work surface and gather into a flat ball. There should still be pieces of butter visible. If the butter is soft, refrigerate the dough for 30 minutes or longer before proceeding.
❸ Roll out the dough into a long rectangle about 16 x 6 inches. Fold in thirds, bringing one side over to cover the middle, then the other on top of it, like folding a letter. Roll again into a long rectangle and fold again the same way (these are called "turns"). Refrigerate the dough for 30 minutes to chill.
❹ Roll out the dough into a long rectangle as before, sprinkle with about one-third of the cheese and fold in thirds. Repeat twice, sprinkling the dough each time with one-third of the cheese. Refigerate the dough, well wrapped, for at least 30 minutes or up to 3 days before using.
❺ Preheat the oven to 425°F. On a lightly floured cool work surface, roll out the dough to a thickness of ⅜ inch, brush lightly with egg and sprinkle with Parmesan. Using a long sharp knife, cut the dough into long thin sticks about ⅜ inch wide by 3 inches long. Place about 1 inch apart on large non-stick baking sheets and bake for 8–10 minutes until they are golden brown.

Variation

If time is short, use 1 pound ready-made puff pastry and fold cheese into it as described in the last two steps.

PARMESAN PUFFS

These little cheesy cream puffs are wonderful to garnish consommé or plain tomato soup. It is difficult to make a really small quantity of the dough, so enjoy the leftovers with a glass of wine – as they do in Burgundy.

MAKES 50-60

½ cup flour
pinch of salt
pinch of freshly grated nutmeg
3 eggs
½ cup water
4 tablespoons unsalted butter, cut in 6 pieces
2 tablespoons freshly grated Parmesan cheese

❶ Preheat the oven to 400°F. Lightly grease a large baking sheet.
❷ Sift together the flour, salt and nutmeg. Beat the eggs in a small bowl.
❸ Bring the water and butter to a boil in a small saucepan. When the butter has melted, remove from the heat and add the sifted dry ingredients all at once. Beat with a wooden spoon until well incorporated and the mixture starts to pull away from the sides of the pan.
❹ Set the pan over low heat and cook the mixture for 1 minute to dry it, stirring constantly.
❺ Off the heat, add about two-thirds of the beaten egg, beat thoroughly with a wooden spoon, then add a little more and beat to incorporate thoroughly. The dough should be smooth and shiny. Drop a little from the spoon; it should pull away and fall slowly. If it does not, add more beaten egg until the dough will drop slowly from the spoon. Stir in the cheese.
❻ Spoon the pastry into a piping bag fitted with a ½-inch plain tip and pipe the dough on the baking sheet in small mounds about ½ inch in diameter and about 1½ inches apart. Alternatively, using a small teaspoon, drop the dough in small mounds. Bake for 15–18 minutes until the puffs are well browned. Allow to cool in the turned-off oven with the door ajar.

Other Garnishes

SPICY GARLIC MAYONNAISE

(*Rouille*)

This sauce, typically served with certain regional fish soups in France, takes its name from the rust color that the pimiento, or roasted red pepper, gives it. Try it also to accompany cold turkey, chicken or shellfish, or to dress a pasta salad.

MAKES ABOUT ¾ CUP

⅔ *cup soft white bread crumbs*
1–2 *garlic cloves, very finely chopped*
1 *egg yolk, at room temperature*

½ *pimiento*
1 *teaspoon tomato paste*
¾ *cup extra-virgin olive oil*

❶ Soak the bread crumbs in warm water and squeeze dry. Put in a food processor with the garlic, egg yolk, pimiento and tomato paste, and purée until smooth. With the machine running, slowly pour the oil through the feed tube, scraping down the sides as needed.
❷ Scrape into a serving dish or storage container. If not using immediately, cover and refrigerate for up to 2 days.

Variations

AIOLI   See Garlic Fish Soup, page 84.
BASIL PUREE   See Provençal Vegetable Soup, page 22.

CRISPY FRIED ONIONS

These crispy onions make an unusual garnish for creamy vegetable soups, but they are also good with sautéed or grilled poultry or meat. Several large shallots may be substituted for the onion.

MAKES ABOUT 6 SERVINGS

1 *large red or yellow onion*
olive or peanut oil, for frying

salt, for sprinkling
(optional)

❶ Cut the onion in half through the stem and remove the root end. Place cut-side down and slice very thinly. Blot the slices on paper towels.
❷ Heat oil to a depth of about ½ inch in a small deep frying pan over medium-high heat until it begins to smoke. Drop in about one-third of the onion slices and fry until deep golden brown. Using a slotted spoon, transfer to paper towels and drain. Cook the remaining onion slices in batches and drain. Sprinkle the onions lightly with salt, if you wish.

DUMPLINGS

CHICKEN QUENELLES   See Tarragon Chicken Consommé with Chicken Quenelles, page 117.
FISH QUENELLES   Substitute 7 ounces boneless white fish fillet for the chicken and parsley for the tarragon.
HERB DUMPLINGS   See Chicken Soup with Herb Dumplings, page 61.
LIVER DUMPLINGS   See Pheasant Soup with Liver Dumplings, page 65.

PASTA

RAVIOLI   See Seafood Ravioli in Bouillon and variations, page 116.
WONTONS   See Wonton Soup, page 113. The filling may also be used for ravioli.
NOODLES   See Chicken Soup with Homemade Noodles, page 64.

INDEX

ACKNOWLEDGEMENTS

Pictor 6, 8–9, Stuart Frawley/Ace 11, Pictor 17, PictureBank 18–19, 21, Mauritius/Ace 23, PictureBank 40–1, Fotopic/Ace 42, Trevor Wood/Image Bank 57, PictureBank 68–9, 70, Zephyr Pictures/Ace 86–7, Allan Stone/Ace 88, Mauritius/Ace 89, Grant V. Faint/Image Bank 98–9, Pictor 100, 108–9, 111, Alan Spence/Ace 118–9, Pictor 120, 122.

All other photographs are the copyright of Quarto Publishing plc.

Quarto would also like to thank Lee Pattison and Villeroy & Boch Tableware Ltd, 267 Merton Road, London SW18 5JS; Oddbins UK Ltd, 31 Weir Road Industrial Estate, London SW19 8UG and Agadir Restaurant, 84 Westbourne Grove, London W2 for supplying props for photography.

Author's acknowledgements:

With my sincere thanks to Beverly Le Blanc and Philip Back for help with recipe testing, Jessica Palmer for her invaluable input on many levels, and most of all to my husband Tim Garland, for his patience with a steady diet of soup, his thoughtful critical analysis and his fine palate.